Child Sexual Abuse

This book aims to critically evaluate the development of policy and legislative measures to control sex offenders. The last 15 years has seen increasing concern on the part of the government, criminal justice agencies, the media and the public regarding child sexual abuse. This concern has been prompted by a series of events including cases inviting media attention and involving the abduction, sexual abuse and murder of young children. The response to this wave of child sexual abuse revelation has been to introduce increasingly punitive legislation regarding the punishment and control of sex offenders – the only group of offenders in British legal history to have their own act – both in custody and in the community. Against the backdrop of a crisis in public confidence regarding the behaviour of child protection professionals, it is argued here that legislation has developed in a reactionary way in response to media and public anxiety regarding the punishment and control of sex offenders, and the perceived threat of such offenders in the community.

Dr Julia C. Davidson is based at the University of Westminster.

Contemporary Issues in Public Policy

Series editors: David Downes and Paul Rock

London School of Economics

This series of books is intended to offer accessible, informed and well-evidenced analyses of topical policy issues – from the national health through women's work to central issues of crime and criminal justice – as a counterweight to the manner in which they tend to be presented in political and public debates. The mass media can be sensationalising and overly-simple. Many observers and commentators are too engaged politically or professionally to take a dispassionate stand. By contrast, what is offered here is considered expert commentary laid out in a literate and helpful manner. Moreover, in the wake of globalisation, the revolution in information technology and new forms of regulation and audit, an immense proliferation of data has occurred which can swamp all but the most experienced and duly sceptical analyst. Providing an excellent core for teaching in social policy, criminology, politics and the sociology of contemporary Britain, the series is also intended for politicians, policy-makers, journalists and other concerned people who wish to know more about the world they live in today.

Other titles in the series:

The Police and Social Conflict
Nigel Fielding

Key Issues in Women's Work
Catherine Hakim

UK Election Law
Bob Watt

Child Sexual Abuse

Media representations and
government reactions

Julia C. Davidson

Routledge·Cavendish
Taylor & Francis Group
a GlassHouse book

First published 2008
by Routledge-Cavendish
2 Park Square, Milton Park, Abingdon, Oxon OX14 5RN

Simultaneously published in the USA and Canada
by Routledge-Cavendish
270 Madison Ave, New York, NY 10016

A GlassHouse book

Routledge-Cavendish is an imprint of the Taylor & Francis Group, an informa business

© 2008 Julia C. Davidson

Typeset in Sabon and Gill Sans by
Florence Production Ltd, Stoodleigh, Devon
Printed and bound in Great Britain by
TJ International, Padstow, Cornwall

British Library Cataloguing in Publication Data
A catalogue record for this book is available from the British Library

Library of Congress Cataloging in Publication Data
Davidson, Julia
    Child sexual abuse: media representations and government reactions/
Julia Davidson.
        p. cm.
    1. Child sexual abuse – Great Britain.   2. Child sexual abuse – Great
    Britain – Government policy.   3. Mass media and crime – Great Britain.
    I. Title.
HV6570.4.G7D38 2008
362.760941—dc22   2007040841

ISBN 10: 1–904385–69–9 (hbk)
ISBN 10: 1–904385–68–0 (pbk)
ISBN 10: 0–203–92873–3 (ebk)

ISBN 13: 978–1–904385–69–1 (hbk)
ISBN 13: 978–1–904385–68–4 (pbk)
ISBN 13: 978–0–203–92873–8 (ebk)

For Glenn, Rhys & my parents
with love and gratitude

Contents

Foreword

In this book, Dr Julia C. Davidson confronts what is now probably the single most emotive topic in the entire criminology field: sexual offenders against children, how they get that way and what is to be done with and about them. It was not always so. While it was the case that the most heinous serial child murders with a sexual character have long aroused the most intensely hostile public reaction – the 'Moors murders' of children by Ian Brady and Myra Hindley in the early 1960s being the most notorious – the spectrum of responses to more common forms of child sex abusers shaded into an indifference to, or even humorous cynicism about, libidinous scoutmasters, public school sadism and 'dirty old men'. Offenders who deviated too far or victimised too often would be institutionally spared public disgrace by private sanctions. Though this relative license may have risked too much, it allowed a 'freedom of the streets' for children that has now been drastically curtailed. For example, in the 1940s and 50s, many parents were content to allow their children to gain entry to 'A' for 'adult' films – basically any film with even a mildly sexual and/or violent element was barred to unaccompanied children under 16 – by asking total strangers to 'take them in'. Such widespread trust would now be unimaginable. Ironically, thanks to far more explicit material now being available to children on home videos, it is also unnecessary.

This example affords a glimpse of a transformation of attitude to child sex offenders which has emerged at a time when the sexualisation of our culture has coincided, and has itself provoked, a heightened sense of risk in relation to sexual victimisation from the extremes of rape to the dangers of child pornography. An aversion to sexual deviance, born in many respects of a deep ambivalence towards the commercialisation of sex, in some ways an unwanted by-product of the virtues of overcoming literary and artistic censorship, has now proliferated into a vastly extended range of measures against sex offenders in general and the sexual victimisation of children in particular. A panoply of adverse labelling extends from more severe sentencing of convicted offenders to their lifelong social exclusion. The expansion of preventive measures, due in part to the woeful neglect of child protection in the past, now includes, as well as demands for the publicisation of the addresses of known child sex offenders, such processes as regular checks on the criminal records of all teachers and staff engaged in primary or secondary education. How far this reaction amounts to an over-reaction, which has counter-productive implications for the very object of the exercise – the protection of children – is now a pressing issue in public policy debate.

This book is therefore a timely and a much-needed assessment of the issues and evidence relating to the definition, causes, character and control of child sex offending in its myriad forms. The author subjects the rapidly growing body of evidence on this emotionally fraught subject to a scrupulous and humane yet dispassionate analysis. The spectres of Ian Huntley and Roy Whiting are the nightmares of every parent. How far nightmares should be not just the starting point but the very basis for criminal justice and public policy is a major theme of this book.

David Downes and Paul Rock
(London School of Economics)
July 2007

Abbreviations

ABE	Achieving Best Evidence
ACLU	American Civil Liberties Union
ASBO	Anti-social Behaviour Order
ATSA	Association for the Treatment of Sexual Abusers
CBT	Cognitive Behavioural Treatment
CEOP	Child Exploitation and Online Protection Centre
CJA	Criminal Justice Act
COPINE	Combating of Paedophile Information Networks in Europe
CPO	Community Punishment Order
CPS	Crown Prosecution Service
DfES	Department for Education and Skills
ECPAT	End Child Prostitution, Child Pornography and Trafficking of Children for Sexual Purposes
IBAQ	Internet Behaviour and Attitudes Questionnaire
i-SOTP	Internet Sex Offender Programme
IWF	Internet Watch Foundation
MAPPA	Multi-Agency Public Protection Agency
NACDL	National Association of Criminal Defense Lawyers
NOMS	National Offender Management Service
NSPCC	National Society for the Prevention of Cruelty to Children
OASys	Offender Assessment System
OLR	Order of Lifelong Restriction
PMOS	Prime Minister's Official Spokesman
RMA	Risk Management Authority
SAP	Sentencing Advisory Panel
SOPO	Sexual Offences Prevention Order

SOPSS   Sex Offender Psychometric System
SOTP   Sex Offender Treatment Programme
USI   Unlawful Sexual Intercourse

Acknowledgements

Thanks to David and Paul for making this book possible and for their patience in guiding me through the process. Thanks to all those academics and practitioners working in this difficult area whose work is referred to in this book.

Chapter 1

Definitions and images of childhood and abuse

This chapter seeks to:

- Define what is meant by 'childhood', exploring historical and legal definitions in the context of consent to sexual relations.

- Provide a critical overview of legal definitions of child sexual abuse.

- Consider the victim's perspective in defining child sexual abuse.

- Explore the prevalence of child sexual abuse with reference to official estimates and victim surveys, both in the 'real world' and in 'cyberspace'.

This chapter begins by exploring what is meant by the concept of childhood and how definitions have changed over time. This is an important first step in defining child sexual abuse, as the transition from childhood to adulthood is inextricably linked with human sexuality and the perceived ability to develop informed consent to sexual relations.

Many authors have tended to assume a common definition of childhood, but in reality definitions vary across cultures and over time. Perceptions of childhood also vary within cultures: media depictions suggest that young people are sometimes both potential victims of sexual and physical assault in need of state protection and an anti-social element in need of social control; a small army of unsupervised, hooded yobs, or 'hoodies', who constitute a threat to the social order. Media coverage of what might have been known as 'muggings' now focuses on the wearing of hooded sweatshirts by young people – a recent *Daily Mail* headline proclaimed that 'Hoodies Broke Woman's Hip in Holiday Cash Robbery'. The *Mail* went on to inform its readers how a 94-year-old woman's hip was broken and her savings stolen (*Daily Mail*, 30 January 2007) – and was the *Mirror* really reflecting the nations fear when it proclaimed 'We Fear our Teens: Britons too Scared to Tackle Hoodies' (23 October 2006)? Such reporting has made wearing hooded sweatshirts, an item of clothing worn by almost every teenager, synonymous with crime and anti-social behaviour.

Legislation introduced by the government over the past five years reflects this contradictory image of children and young people: two consecutive Children Acts (1989 and 2004) have sought to empower children, allowing them a hitherto unheard voice as victims, in family welfare proceedings and other matters that concern their future. Children and young people have been afforded the right to express a view and to have that view taken into account by professionals working on their behalf in the criminal justice system. In the wake of the Children Act 2004 and the National Framework (Every Child Matters: Change for Children) the latest research seeks to explore children's perceptions about professional practice in an effort to make practice more child-centred.[1]

The introduction of anti-social behaviour orders (ASBOs) presents a rather different image, seeking to both control and restrict the behaviour of young people. ASBOs are civil orders that set out conditions regarding behaviour: they can be applied for by the police, social services and registered social landlords. The vast majority of these orders are made against young people under the age of 18. In the five-year period from April 1999, 2,455 ASBOs were granted; in 2006 alone the figure was 9,853 (Home Office, 2006), a steep increase. Such measures constitute a direct attempt to control a group of young adolescents who are viewed as out of control and lacking in parental supervision. It did not take long for the media to begin questioning the worth of the ASBO: '55% of Asbos Broken' said the *Mirror* (7 December 2006), commenting that 'Labour's high-profile crackdown on yobs is failing with more than half of all anti-social

---

1   See research undertaken by the author, for example Davidson et al. (2006) and Plotnikoff and Woolfson (2004).

behaviour orders being breached, it emerged yesterday. One critic blasted the system, saying the louts were "sneering at the authorities"'. The *Guardian* ran a story indicating surprise that a young person given an ASBO had suggested that it had made a positive impact on his life (20 December 2006).

If social policy reflects a society's view about key issues, UK social policy over the last five years is quite unclear both how childhood is to be viewed and how children are to be treated. It is also unclear where childhood ends and adulthood begins: current perceptions of childhood are relatively recently created constructs. Aries (1962) claims that children were not portrayed at all in art until the twelfth century as the concept of childhood did not exist in the same sense; in a similar fashion to other mammals, children were considered independent and by definition adult from an early age. This view of childhood extended long beyond medieval times: note for example the manner in which working-class children were expected to undertake what would today be considered adult labour from a young age, a trend that continued right up until the end of the nineteenth century.[2]

Indeed children were exploited as a workforce during the industrial revolution: their small, light physical frames were suited to many jobs that adults were unable or unwilling to undertake. Children were in demand for work in the mines and as chimney sweeps, for example, but were also used as domestic labour in their own homes and in others' homes. As Thompson (1982) suggests 'Child labour was not new. The child was an intrinsic part of the agricultural and industrial economy before 1780, and remained so until rescued by school' (p 367). It would seem that the advent of formal education did more than 'rescue' poor children from hard labour; it helped to reinvent and redefine our sense of childhood.

Coveney (1982) suggests that children did not appear to any significant extent in English literature until the end of the eighteenth century, though this may be more to do with a tendency on the part

---

2   The author's grandmother (92 at the time of writing) recounts an early experience when as a 13-year-old she was sent from her home in South Wales to work as a scullery maid for a wealthy family in London that she had never met before. Although difficult this seemed 'normal' at the time as she was no longer considered to be a child and her earnings would have been an essential part of the family income. She worked long hours and a seven-day week (with two hours free on a Sunday morning to attend church) for a low wage.

of historians and writers to ignore children and their experiences rather than being indicative of social perceptions of childhood at a particular point in time. Queen Victoria reputedly remarked that 'children should be seen and not heard', and their disempowered voices are largely absent from many historical accounts. DeMause (1982) claims that historians have tended to focus upon 'fantastic castles' and 'magnificent battles' (p 48) neglecting playgrounds and the home. It is in reality the case that children have historically been considered politically and economically important only insofar as they were able to serve adult needs; working class children constituted a large army of easily manipulated, exploitable labour with no rights and no political voice.

Jenks (1996) suggests that it is preferable to speak of 'childhoods' rather than 'childhood', given the diversity of experience and expectation that comprises our early lives both historically and culturally. It is further argued that our common understanding of childhood within a particular social structure is brought about through the establishment of rituals, values and organisations that focus upon children and guide their early lives. During the twenty-first century childhood has become a recognised state extending well into adolescence, around which a large social welfare, educational and commercial industry has grown.

Consent to sexual relations: the end of childhood

Although it is difficult to define precisely when a person ceases to be a child, the law in England and Wales (Sexual Offences Act 2003, s 9) is clear in regarding 16 years as being the age at which a person can give informed consent to both hetero- and homosexual activity.[3]

---

3   The age of consent to homosexual sexual relations has recently been lowered to 16 (from 21 in England and Wales under the Sexual Offences Act 1967, s 1, amended by the UK Criminal Justice and Public Order Act 1994, s 145, which lowered the age to 18) following pressure from gay rights groups such as Outrage. The present Labour Government tabled an amendment to the Sexual Offences Act 1956 to lower the age of consent from 18 to 16, the second reading received a government majority of 183 votes (313 to 130 votes). The Lords, however, rejected the bill at this time. It was then decided on a free vote (by 263 to 102 votes) to provide parity between the age of consent to heterosexual and homosexual relations. This move forms a part of the Sexual Offences (Amendment) Act 2000.

As sexual activity is associated with adulthood and maturity in western society, the age at which a person can give consent to sexual relations implies the end of childhood. Children and young people are seen to lack the capacity or 'competence' (Children Acts 1989, 2004) to make a sound judgement about sexual relations: as Finkelhor suggests, 'children are deemed to lack the capacity to consent to such relationships. However, at some point in adolescence children acquire the ability to consent' (1984, p 26). The age of consent has steadily increased over time, reflecting both the manner in which perceptions of childhood have changed and the extension of the state of childhood. In Scotland, England and Wales the age of consent to heterosexual sexual relations was 10 in the year 1285, rising to 13 in 1875 and was eventually set at 16 in 1885 in the Criminal Law Amendment Act. This is comparable to some other countries, such as Switzerland, New Zealand and the United States. There are however differences – there is a government move in Romania, for example, to lower the age of consent from 15 to 13. This has provoked outrage among child welfare groups in Western Europe (Roth-Szamoskozi, 2000), who are opposing the move. The age of consent has been set at 14 in Canada since 1892 (with extra protection for children abused by perpetrators in a position of trust where the age of consent is raised to 18) and is similarly 14 in Portugal and in Brazil. In India the law is contradictory: the paediatric or medical age at which childhood ends is 12 and currently no child abuse legislation exists; the 'Offences Against The Child Bill', which sought to address this issue, has been rejected by the Law Ministry on the grounds that it overlapped with child protection provisions in other legislation (Chauhan, 2007). Chauhan suggests that this move constitutes a major blow to the Women Child and Development Ministry. However, the difficulty is that marriages involving under-15s are still commonplace. In South Africa the age of consent for boys was set at 19 in an attempt to curb the increasing HIV problem among young people, high teenage pregnancy rates and the high rate of adolescent rape:

> Childhood in South Africa is seriously compromised by the HIV/AIDS pandemic and we also have very high levels of early teenage pregnancy. The age of first sexual experience has also dropped with a significant percentage of children having their first sexual experience between the age of 10 and 13 years. South

Africa also has the dubious reputation of having the highest incidence of rape per 100,000 of the population, with 50 per cent of all victims being children. Politicians who were motivating for the age of 18 years believed that this would protect our youth from early pregnancies and HIV/AIDS infection. Submissions to the Parliamentary Portfolio Committee on Justice and Constitutional Development strongly supported the age of consent to sexual relationships remaining at 16 for both genders.

(Van Niekerk, 2007)

As a consequence the Criminal Law (Sexual Offences and Related Matters) Amendment Bill was passed in the House of Assembly in South Africa on 22 May 2007. The age of consent is now set at 16 years for both boys and girls. However, children engaging in sexual relations could possibly be criminalised under this new legislation, as both will be charged with an offence. Research with young people aged 13–16 undertaken in South Africa by Peterson et al. (2005) suggests that several issues give rise to high levels of sexual violence among adolescents, including:

- the prevailing culture of masculinity and the right of males to domination over females;
- the normalisation of violence and poverty;
- poor community management/control of adolescents;
- low adolescent self esteem and life chances among the poor.

The authors conclude that prevention and education programmes should be set up for adolescents that address all of these issues.

Differences in the age of consent to sexual relations reflect social, cultural, political and religious differences in views about the nature and end of childhood. In some countries such as India, where traditionally children have married at what would be considered a young age in western societies, the debate regarding child abuse and the age of consent is recent and developing. In other countries such as South Africa the setting of the age of consent has been driven by moves to curb disease, pregnancy and sexual violence among young people.

The age of criminal responsibility is still however set at ten years in England and Wales and eight in Scotland, this despite the adoption of the welfare-based court system in the UK. In most Western

European countries the age of criminal responsibility is between 13 and 16, and is comparable to the age of consent. The UN Committee on the Rights of the Child recommended that the age of criminal responsibility should be raised in the UK. The age of criminal responsibility in New Zealand is also ten, however, children under the age of 14 can only be prosecuted for the offences of murder and manslaughter (End Child Prostitution, Child Pornography and Trafficking of Children for Sexual Purposes (ECPAT), 2007). In recent research conducted by Allen (2006) on behalf of the Centre for Crime and Justice Studies, it is suggested that the low age of criminal responsibility serves to demonise and criminalise children in the UK. Allen suggests a shift away from the punitive approach to a way that seeks to address the health, family and educational difficulties that often underlie such offending. An overhaul of the youth justice system is recommended by Allen: 'We have seen an increasing pre-occupation with protecting the public from young people and a growing intolerance of teenage misbehaviour of all kinds. A genuine shift from punishment to problem solving as the guiding principle for tackling youth crime would help to produce a society that is both safer and fairer' (Allen, 2006).

In the UK the age of consent was increased in Victorian England following concerns about the level of child prostitution raised by campaigners such as Bramwell Booth from the Salvation Army and William Stead, the editor of the *Pall Mall Gazette*. Prior to the advent of the Criminal Law Amendment Act in 1885, Stead published four articles describing the plight of child prostitutes in Victorian England. The series of articles was entitled 'The Maiden Tribute Of Modern Babylon', and described in some detail the ease with which he had purchased a child prostitute.[4] The Act was passed shortly afterwards and ironically Stead, along with five others, was charged with unlawfully kidnapping a minor and was imprisoned for three months in Holloway Gaol (Autograph Letter Collection). At the time, the penalty for sexual activity with a female under 14 was life imprisonment: 'any person who unlawfully and carnally knows any girl under the age of 14 years shall be guilty of felony, and being convicted thereof shall be liable to be kept in penal servitude for life' (Home Office, 2007).

It is clear that definitions and perceptions of childhood have changed enormously over time. The concept of an age of consent was

---

4   The child, Eliza Armstrong, was the 13-year-old daughter of a chimney sweep.

not introduced into English law until 1285; until the late-thirteenth century it was legally possible for an adult to have sexual relations with a 10-year-old child. Legislation does not occur in a vacuum but rather reflects the social context in which it develops. Western society has become more child-centred, and it is no longer acceptable to abuse and exploit children, physically, sexually or economically. The Children Act 2004 builds upon the EU Convention on the Rights of the Child[5] in attempting to give children a voice, which hitherto has been unheard. The EU Convention sets out the basic rights of children and young people under 18. The Convention requires Member States to ensure that these rights are enshrined in law; it was ratified in the UK in 1991, and a condition of ratification is that States must develop a programme of monitoring and report to the EU on progress made on a regular basis (two years following ratification and every five years thereafter) (Foreign and Commonwealth Office, 2005). Following the EU Convention several themes are emphasised in the Children Act 2004 and are taken up in the framework. These are: the health and safety of children; enjoyment and achievement; making a positive contribution and economic well being.

Child sexual abuse: legal definitions

The Sexual Offences Act 1956 laid the foundation for more recent legislation, such as the Sexual Offences Act 2003. In the 1956 Act notifiable sexual offences were classified into separate categories including: unlawful sexual intercourse (USI) with a girl under 13; unlawful sexual intercourse with a girl under 16 (over 13); gross indecency with a child; rape; indecent assault on a male; indecent assault on a female; indecency between males; procuration; abduction; bigamy and incest.

The list incorporated offences which are clearly sexually motivated and involve the commission of a sexual act or acts against adults and children, for example gross indecency with a child and rape. The definition also included offences which may be sexually motivated but do not involve the commission of a sexual act, for

---

5   The Convention builds upon the Universal Declaration of Human Rights, which points to the vulnerable position of children and the need for special care and attention.

Rape and other sexual offences against children under 13 (ss 5–8)

Child sex offences (ss 9–15)

Abuse of position of trust (ss 16–24)

Familial child sex offences (ss 25–29)

Indecent photographs of children (ss 45–46)

Abuse of children through prostitution and pornography (ss 47–49).

Figure 1.1 Sexual offences against children – The Sexual Offences Act 2003

example abduction. At the same time some offences which were clearly sexually motivated, such as indecent exposure, were excluded. So were any number of offences that involved sexual abuse but may have been classified in a different way: violent offences involving the commission of a sexual offence for example (Howard League, 1985). The limited and ambiguous use of such categories had major implications both for what came to be defined as a sexual offence and for the measurement of the incidence of sexual offending.

The Sexual Offences Act 2003 (Figure 1.1) clarifies the position with regard to the sexual abuse of children, outlining several distinct offence categories, which now form the basis of the Home Office statistics. These are: rape and other offences against children (ss 5–8)[6]; child sex offences (which includes the new offence of 'meeting a child following sexual grooming', s 15); abuse of position of trust (ss 16–24, following the Sexual Offences Amendment Act 2000); familial child sex offences (ss 25–29); indecent photographs of children (ss 45–46); and abuse of children through prostitution and pornography (ss 47–49). Other sections of the Act also have an impact upon children: sections 57–68 deal with trafficking offences to the UK for sexual exploitation, for example. Key changes in the legislation are discussed below.

6 A distinction is made in ss 5–8 between the rape of a child under 13 and the assault of a child under 13 by penetration: the key difference being that the latter includes vaginal and oral sex (previously categorised as 'indecent assault' under the Sexual Offences Act 1956, and therefore carrying a more lenient sentence). The maximum sentence for both offences is now life imprisonment.

> 1 A looks after persons under 18 who are detained in an institution;
>
> 2 A looks after persons under 18 who are resident in a home (local authority or voluntary organisation);
>
> 3 A looks after persons under 18 who are accommodated and cared for in a hospital, residential care home, mental nursing home, community home or children's home;
>
> 4 A looks after persons under 18 who are receiving full-time education at an educational institution, and B is receiving such education at that institution.

Figure 1.2 Sexual Offences (Amendment) Act 2000 – position of trust
Source: Home Office, 2007

Position of trust

The Labour Government introduced the concept of 'position of trust' into English and Welsh law, via the Sexual Offences (Amendment) Act 2000 (ss 3–4).[7] The act raised the age of consent to under 18 where the alleged perpetrator is in a position of trust with regard to the victim. This includes social workers, teachers and doctors, for example. The definition of 'position of trust' is set out in Figure 1.2.

Sexual grooming and indecent internet images of children

A new offence category was created in the Sexual Offences Act 2003: section 15 makes 'meeting a child following sexual grooming'[8] an offence, which applies to the internet, other technologies such as mobile phones and to the 'real world'. Another offence category 'indecent photographs of children' (ss 45–46) is included in the legislation in an attempt to address the trade in indecent images of children on the internet. The Internet Watch Foundation (IWF) have reported a rise in the number of websites containing indecent

---

7 Now incorporated into the Sexual Offences Act 2003.
8 The Home Office defines grooming as 'a course of conduct enacted by a suspected paedophile, which would give a reasonable person cause for concern that any meeting with a child arising from the conduct would be for unlawful purposes' (Home Office, 2002). This definition formed the basis of the grooming clause in the Sexual Offences Act 2003.

United States 51%

Russia 20%

Spain 7%

Japan 5%

United Kingdom 1.6%

Figure 1.3 Internet Watch Foundation – origin of websites containing child abuse images 1996–2006
Source: Internet Watch Foundation 2006

images of children, from 3,438 in 2004 to 6,000 in 2006. The vast majority of the websites are hosted outside of the UK and are therefore difficult to police (Figure 1.3). Recent statistics produced by the IWF suggest that 615 reports of internet abuse were received during their first year of operation (1996), compared to 27,750 reports in 2006 (85 per cent of which related to suspected child abuse websites). During the ten-year period, 31,000 websites have been found to contain potentially illegal child abuse images. It is claimed that the number of reported websites containing illegal child abuse images has fallen in the UK from 18 per cent in 1996 to 0.2 per cent in 2006.

Police High Technology Crime Units currently investigate the grooming of children on the internet and indecent online images of children. Following Operation Ore successful prosecutions have been brought under the Act both for 'grooming' online and for the possession of indecent internet images. This police operation was launched on the basis of information provided to the police by the FBI, regarding 7,200 men who had allegedly accessed pay-per-view websites and shared peer-to-peer technology in sharing indecent images of children. The National Crime Squad (which targets serious and violent crime) has made several thousand convictions since 2002 under Operation Ore.

'Grooming' involves a process of socialisation during which an offender seeks to interact with a child (and sometimes the child's family), possibly sharing their hobbies, interests and computer slang in an attempt to gain trust in order to prepare them for sexual abuse. A Probation Officer participating in recent research commented:

I've worked with men who've spent months preparing a child for abuse online before meeting up with them. The lengths they will go to are extraordinary. I knew one man who spent a long time online learning children's computing language so that he could communicate more effectively and present himself as a child. He would spend time in chat rooms learning how children talk to each other and then go online to see if he was convincing. After a lot of test runs eventually he was convincing.

(Probation Officer, National Probation Service, 2006, cited in Davidson, 2007)

The process may also involve an attempt to persuade a child that sexual relations between adults and children are acceptable. Several countries are beginning to follow the UK lead in legislating against 'grooming' behaviour. Scotland followed the English lead when a similar clause was introduced into Scottish legislation in 2005. The Protection of Children and Prevention of Sexual Offences (Scotland) Act 2005 includes a clause covering 'meeting a child following certain preliminary contact' (s 1), the English equivalent of 'grooming'. Sexual grooming has also recently been added to the Crimes Amendment Act 2005 in New Zealand. In the United States it is an offence to electronically transmit information about a child aged under 16 for the purpose of committing a sexual offence (US Code: Title 18, Part 1, Chapter 117, AS 2425). The Australian Criminal Code (s 218A) makes similar restrictions, as does the Canadian Criminal Code (s 172.1). The UK legislation differs in that the sexual grooming offence applies both to cyberspace and to the 'real world'; legislation in other countries addresses only electronic grooming via the internet and mobile phones. In reality it would be extremely difficult to police and gather evidence on grooming behaviour in the 'real world'; it is therefore unsurprising that no cases have been brought to court on this basis under the Sexual Offences Act 2003.

The concept of sexual grooming has in reality been drawn from the sex offender literature, where it is well documented (Finkelhor et al., 1986; Beech et al., 1998), into legislation, and is now filtering into crime prevention initiatives. For example, the recently launched (April 2006) government-funded Child Exploitation and Online Protection Centre (CEOP, 2006), an organisation involving the police and other criminal justice agencies in 'tackling' online abuse, and which draws upon expertise from internet service providers such as AOL and Microsoft and children's charities such as the National Society for the Prevention of Cruelty to Children (NSPCC). This new centre aims to raise awareness among children and parents about the potential dangers of the internet; create a database of known offenders; and allow officers to police chat rooms posing as children in order to detect any grooming behaviour. Fake websites will be set up to attract sex offenders. These policing tactics are not new: the High Technology Crime Unit at New Scotland Yard has placed undercover officers in teen and other chat rooms likely to attract children since the introduction of the Sexual Offences Act 2003. These officers have learnt to interact as children do online (Davidson and Martellozzo, 2004), through the use of text language in order to prompt and encourage conversation with child abusers seeking to groom a child. Several recent convictions have been secured on this basis.

School-based programmes aiming to educate children about the dangers posed by sex offenders in cyberspace are now routinely delivered to secondary school children and their parents in the UK and other countries such as New Zealand and Canada (Davidson and Martellozzo, 2004). Internet service providers have also taken some action to address child safety in internet chat rooms: British Telecom introduced Operation 'CleanFeed' in 2003, shocking the industry by using a list of sites (provided by the IWF) which have been frequently found to contain illegal and indecent material and blocking them at server level following concerns over sex offenders use of the service to target children (Galvin, IPPR, 2004). Other internet service providers such as MSN and Yahoo[9] have taken some action to protect children in chat rooms, but undoubtedly more could be done. In the United States an attempt to sue the popular peer-to-peer network Myspace for $30 million has recently been launched by attorneys representing the parents of children who were groomed and sexually abused by men they met on the network. The negligence and fraud suit claims that Myspace should take responsibility as the teenagers' profiles were easily viewed, there being currently no age verification system, and adults are easily able to present themselves as teenagers. Thirty-three state attorneys in the United States are presently trying to force Myspace to increase the minimum age to 16 (it is currently 14) and to cross-check ages against the national

9   Yahoo were forced into action in 2005 by a New York State Attorney General's Office investigation which found that users were creating chatrooms explicitly for the purpose of grooming children for abuse. Yahoo then agreed to put into place procedures to ensure that the creation of such chatrooms would not continue (Attorney General, 2005).

database for verification. Myspace has responded through plans to introduce Project 'Zephyr' in late 2007/early 2008, software that will alert parents of the age and details entered into their child's profile (Kelly, 2007). Companies such as Myspace do currently provide internet safety information on their websites aimed at children and parents but, should this case be successful, internet service providers will have to become more actively engaged with their young users, schools and parents in raising awareness about internet safety, or many other such cases will follow.

Informed consent

Arguably the single most important point to be established in English law by the Sexual Offences Act 2003 is that children under 13 lack the capacity to consent to sexual relations. Government guidance states: 'whether or not the child consented to this act is irrelevant' (Home Office, 2004). Under the previous legislation (Sexual Offences Act 1956) defence barristers could (and did) argue successfully that a child's behaviour or dress was in some way provocative and their behaviour consensual. Consent is no longer an issue to be debated in court where the victim is under 13 years of age.

However, consent remains a somewhat grey area where a child is 14 or 15 years of age: section 9 of the Sexual Offences Act 2003 (Sexual Activity With A Child) states that a sexual offence occurs where the victim is under 13 or 'is under 16 and A (the perpetrator) does not reasonably believe that B (the victim) is 16 or over'. Therefore the burden of proof rests with the prosecution in such cases: 'where the child is aged 13 or over but under 16, the prosecution must prove that A (the perpetrator) did not reasonably believe that he the victim) was 16 or over'. This is something of an anomaly: while the law is clear regarding the age of consent, the suggestion here is that some 'children' of 13 and above may look like young adults and may actively encourage abuse through deception regarding their true age. This may well prove to be an effective defence in court.

The Act also addresses the possibility that a mutually consenting sexual relationship between a 17-year-old and a 15-year-old could have been criminalised under the Sexual Offences Act 1956. Ashworth (1999) states that in reality, under the old legislation, the Crown Prosecution Service reserved prosecution for cases where the relationship was clearly abusive. However, under the new legislation the perpetrators age is raised to 18 and over. This does of course raise questions about the real difference between the motivations and sexual maturity of a 17-year-old compared to those of an 18-year-old, but a legal line must presumably be drawn somewhere.

It is clear that inaccuracies and anomalies have been built into official definitions of what constitutes a sexual offence and the issue of informed consent in the past. The way in which a sexual offence against a child has been categorised under previous legislation has been something of a lottery (Ashworth, 1999) and broad categories such as indecent assault (Sexual Offences Act 1956) have told us little about the nature or the severity of the offending. While the Sexual Offences Act 2003 has introduced a more detailed and comprehensive list of offence categories pertaining to the sexual abuse of children, certain anomalies remain: the 'position of trust' concept appears to extend childhood further in law in recognition of the fact that some young people under 18 may be vulnerable and in need of protection. This concept is reinforced by both Children Acts (1989 and 2004) where young people are considered to be 'children' in need of legal protection until under the age of 18. However, the introduction of a baseline of over 13 years to 'consent' seems to contradict this assertion. Is the key message of the new legislation really that although the legal age of consent is 16, children aged 13 and above (with certain exceptions) have the capacity to consent to sexual activity? The legislation falls short of fully tackling the consent issue for this reason, and sends a clear message to sentencers and defence barristers that child victims of 13 and above are to be viewed differently from younger children in law, and may be treated differently in criminal proceedings. The legislation therefore does little to clarify definitions of childhood and much to confuse the issue.

Defining abuse: how harmful is abuse? Victims' perceptions and experiences

The literature is divided regarding the extent of harm caused by sexual abuse. Wyatt and Powell (1988) in their review of the literature distinguish between the short-term and long-term effects of abuse. Initial effects are characterised as fear, depression, anxiety, anger, guilt and sexually inappropriate behaviour. Long-term effects are said to be isolation and stigmatisation; poor self esteem; lack of trust; and difficulty in conducting adult relationships. The presence and extent of such psychological and emotional problems may depend upon the nature and extent of the abuse experienced; indeed Wyatt and Powell go on to state that sexual abuse perpetrated by fathers or stepfathers involving genital contact and the use of force has the most disturbing consequences for children. Clearly, sustained and frequent abuse, perpetrated by a person who knows a child, will probably be more damaging than a single incident, as this involves an abuse of trust.

Research exploring the victim's perspective (Finkelhor, 1984; Salter, 1988; Morrison et al., 1994; Carter, 1999; Davidson 2006) indicates that in the vast majority of cases where a child has been subject to sexual abuse on the part of an adult it was a negative and frightening experience for the victim, resulting in long-term behavioural and emotional problems. Research conducted by Roberts (1993) sheds further light on the victim's experience. In a qualitative study (employing in-depth interviewing) of 84 sexually abused children she found that one year after the abuse ceased children were still very much in fear of the perpetrator and extremely emotionally affected by the abuse.

A North American study conducted by Doyle-Peters (1988), with a sample of 126 black women and 122 white women, suggests that in both groups sexual abuse had a much greater impact where sustained and/or serious contact was involved. Such women were more likely to be depressed and to have a history of substance misuse. An unusual victim study, which supports the findings of Doyle-Peters' work, was conducted by Briere and Runtz (1986, 1988) in a Canadian health centre. Of 152 women seeking counselling, 67 (44.1 per cent) had experienced sexual abuse in childhood (defined here as any sexual contact under 15 years of age, with a person at least five years older). This group of women was compared to those not experiencing sexual abuse, though it should be noted that the majority of the women (from both groups) had experienced physical abuse in childhood. The findings suggest that those experiencing sexual abuse were more likely to have taken medication for a mental health problem; more likely to have made a suicide attempt; more likely to have an eating disorder; and more likely to have a history of substance misuse than those who had not experienced sexual abuse. The abused group were also more likely to report feelings of self-destructiveness and adult sexual problems. So severe were some of these women's symptoms that Briere and Runtz suggest that they may have been suffering from a form of delayed post-traumatic stress disorder. They suggest that the anger displayed by victims mirrors that of rape victims and might be attributable to feelings of helplessness and loss of control that often accompany child sexual abuse. However, the definition of sexual abuse adopted by Briere and Runtz was broad, and it is difficult to believe that all respondents experienced the same difficulties in adult life. The severity of the sexual abuse suffered should have been compared to the nature and extent of the respondents' symptoms. Martin et al. (2004) conducted a survey of 2,485 children from Southern Australia (average age of 14) and found that a history of sexual abuse in childhood increases the likelihood of depression and suicide attempts. This finding is supported by the work of Ystgaard et al. (2004) in Norway, who found a significant link between childhood sexual abuse and physical abuse and repeated suicide attempts. In China, a study exploring the experiences of 2,300 high school children in four provinces found that both male and female respondents who had been sexually abused reported higher rates of depression than those who had not, and that female respondents were more likely to have an eating disorder. The authors conclude that although differences are evident regarding informed consent between Eastern and Western societies, the damaging psychological impact of sexual abuse experienced in childhood is similar (Chen et al., 2004).

Other research addressing the victim's perspective has reached similar conclusions (Salter, 1988; Herman, 1991). Such research has been conducted with known victims and, given that a large amount of abuse remains hidden, it follows that there are many adults who have perhaps never spoken of their victimisation. Summit (1988) suggests that the very fact that many victims feel unable to divulge their experiences says a great deal about a society that is unwilling to listen and believe their accounts. He maintains that society itself is in denial about the extent of sexual abuse perpetrated against children:

> every extended family, every neighbourhood, every church congregation, every medical society, every class in law school and most every football team . . . conceals people who are hiding unspeakable memories of 'unusual' childhood sexual experiences – the fact that they cannot be shared says something about our collective fear of finding out.
>
> (p 57)

Findings from the author's own research (Davidson, 2006) exploring sex offender and victim accounts of the circumstances of offences suggest that rather than willing accomplices to abuse, children were in fear of the perpetrators and disturbed by their behaviour. One 16-year-old victim who had been sexually abused since the age of ten by her grandfather described feelings of 'shame, embarrassment and pain' as a consequence of his actions. Even very young victims in this study expressed a sense of violation and wrongdoing. One 4-year-old victim stated that 'He (abuser) had done a bad thing and I was hurt', while an older victim stated that 'I felt really scared because I thought he (abuser) might try to do it to me every time I went round to him.' Another victim described the abuse suffered as 'horrible' and as 'making me feel sick'. One 18-year-old victim, who successfully brought a case against her stepfather some years after the abuse occurred, described her feelings:

> There were lots of reasons why I didn't say anything to anyone. I was frightened of X, for myself, and for mum and for my sisters. I was worried my mum would believe him rather than me, I just couldn't tell anyone.
>
> (Davidson, 2006)

There is little research exploring experiences of abuse among disabled children; however, one recent study conducted in Norway suggests that hearing-impaired children are more likely to experience sexual abuse. Kvam (2004) undertook a retrospective survey of 1,150 adult members on the Norwegian Deaf Register and compared the findings to a similar survey of the general adult population. The findings indicate that hearing-impaired children are at significantly greater risk of becoming the victims of childhood sexual abuse than hearing children. It is of concern that the findings also suggest that the abuse was more severe and infrequently reported. Research exploring the extent of abuse among such vulnerable children is an important priority.

The experience of child victims in developing countries

Most of the research exploring victims perceptions has been conducted in the United States, Western Europe and Canada, where funding is available. Although a small amount of research has recently been conducted with children in developing countries, where violence and abuse are an everyday occurrence and often take place against a backdrop of social and political unrest and general violence, the views of such children have largely been excluded from the literature. Dunne et al. (2006) suggest that lack of funding is partly to blame, and that there exists an unwillingness on the part of some governments to formally record and document the incidence and nature of child abuse.

Some small-scale research has been undertaken which serves to provide a glimpse into the experiences of some of these children and young people: Miles (2006), in his study of 1,314 Cambodian children's perceptions of violence and abuse, found that 63.5 per cent of females (N = 671) and 64 per cent of males (N = 639) indicated that they knew children who had been raped. Approximately 24 per cent of the total sample had witnessed a rape. These children experienced violence and abuse, as primary and secondary victims, as a part of their everyday lives, but recognised the negative impact and hoped for a different life. Researchers attempting to investigate child victims' experiences in developing countries have encountered difficulties in gaining access. Miles (2006) negotiated with the Cambodian Ministry of Education for 18 months before he was able to access schools. Another study was conducted by Mitra and Deb (2006) with a sample of 160 Indian street children from the metropolitan region of Kolkata. The authors suggest that there are approximately 30.8 million children living in India who have been abandoned by their parents or who are orphaned, many of whom live on the streets. It is not surprising that the primary goal of the children in this research was to survive on a daily basis, often by whatever means necessary. From the sample, 58 per cent of the children reported being abused by a number of people in their lives, including other street children.

The commercial sexual exploitation of children or child trafficking[10] has recently become a large industry, particularly in developing countries. It is often young women and children from poor backgrounds who are trafficked to other countries for the purposes of cheap labour or sexual abuse. The children and their families are often misled regarding the life that awaits them at their destination. There is little research addressing the experiences of trafficked

10 Defined by the United Nations as the use of a child for sexual or other purposes in exchange for payment or favours, between the customer, intermediary or agent and others who profit from the trade in children for these purposes (UN, 2007).

children, but the recent work of Deb and Sen in India (2006) sheds some light upon the issue. In this study the researchers sought the experiences of a small group of 35 trafficked children and young women who had been taken into custody for being trafficked, or forced prostitution, and placed in a residential programme: the authors comment that trafficked children are often criminalised and held to account for their predicament. The majority of the sample were illiterate and from a low socio-economic group. The findings point to high levels of trauma in the sample, and 43 per cent were suffering from post-traumatic stress.

Such studies play an important role in raising awareness about the plight of children living in difficult circumstances, where survival is often a primary consideration and abuse a part of life that must be endured. However, some proponents of children's rights have stated that incidences of abuse and violence should not be tolerated in the context of social unrest and poverty, and that every attempt to address the position of vulnerable children should be made (Bequele, 2006).

If the sexual abuse of children is of no benefit to the victim, and research demonstrates that it is not, then it is clearly conducted for the gratification of the perpetrator. On this theme Morrison et al. (1994) define sexual abuse simply as 'actual or threatened sexual exploitation of a child or adolescent' (1994, p xix). It should be acknowledged that such exploitation now also occurs in cyberspace.

Although legal definitions regarding what constitutes a sexual offence against a child are sometimes imprecise, it is clear that the consequences are often enduring and painful for the victim regardless of their culture and geographical location. Therefore, any definition of what constitutes child sexual abuse must encompass the victim's perspective in recognising that sexual abuse can, and often does, damage children.

The extent of the problem

Prevalence in the 'real' world

It is difficult to know whether the incidence of sexual offending against children has increased, though official criminal statistics indicate that the rate of reporting has increased substantially since the early 1980s. The total number of sexual offences recorded by the police increased by 38 per cent (from 21,107 to 29,004) between 1980 and 1990; the figure increased between 1997 and 2000 from

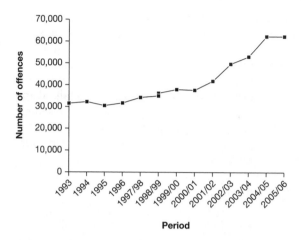

Figure 1.4 'Sexual offences' – long-term national recorded crime trend
Source: Research Development and Statistics (CRCSG), Home Office Crime Statistics for England and Wales, 2006

32,581 to 37,263. In 2005/06, 62,081 sexual offences were recorded (Home Office, 2007, Figure 1.4). The Annual British Crime Survey undertaken by the Home Office provides data collected from a large random sample of the general population regarding their experience of crime; unfortunately children under 16 years of age are excluded from the sample and the incidence of sexual abuse in childhood is not explored.

A breakdown of sexual offences by victim age is not provided in the Home Office criminal statistics. A somewhat out-of-date comparison of Home Office data from 1985 and 1995 is provided by Grubin (1998). The 1985 data excludes the category of rape as no distinction was made then between the rape of adult women and children. This analysis suggests that sexual offences perpetrated against children formed a small proportion of the total number of recorded sexual offences; it is however difficult to establish how far this remains true in 2006. Data on sexual offending from the 2004/05 British Crime Survey[11] suggests that 23 per cent of women and 3 per cent of men reported experiencing sexual abuse after the age of 16. Research conducted by Kelly, Lovett and Regan (2005) suggests that

11   A large-scale survey of the population in England and Wales which seeks to gauge levels of offending by measuring victims' experiences (Home Office, 2007).

45 per cent of rapes and attempted rapes in England and Wales during 2002 were perpetrated against victims under 16. In the same year 1,288 defendants were prosecuted for the rape or attempted rape of a child, 292 (23 per cent) of whom received a conviction (Kelly et al., 2005).

Marshall (1997) suggests that the number of convictions for sexual offences against children continues to increase, when expressed as a proportion of all offences. The number of convictions as a proportion of all recorded sexual offences against children has however fallen significantly. This might suggest reluctance on the part of the Crown Prosecution Service (CPS) to prosecute such cases in the absence of either a guilty plea or conclusive evidence. It is clear that obtaining children's evidence in a form acceptable to a court is extremely difficult, and that disclosure itself is often difficult for victims, although it becomes somewhat easier with age. For example, recent research conducted in Norway suggests that rates of disclosure of sexual abuse increase with victim age, with only 50 per cent of 3–6 year olds disclosing abuse when questioned, compared to 74 per cent of 11–14 year olds (Jensen et al., 2005). Research also concludes that rates of disclosure were lower in intra-familial abuse cases (Davidson et al., 2006).

Research studies employing victim surveys indicate that the problem is much more prevalent than official statistics suggest (Nash and West, 1985; MORI, 1986 and 1988; Cawson, 2000). Child sexual abuse is an offence surrounded by secrecy, which victims may not report for fear of disbelief, or for fear of violent reaction on the part of the perpetrator. This is particularly relevant in the case of abuse within families, where the victim may share a home with the perpetrator. Cawson's (2000) research for the NSPCC indicates that 72 per cent of her sample of adult respondents did not disclose the abuse they endured in childhood and 31 per cent had not disclosed their experiences in adulthood. Research has demonstrated that the loss of control in sexually abusive relationships with adults and fear of being harmed by the perpetrator frequently prevents children from responding to the abuse at the time and from reporting abuse (Summit, 1988). This is reinforced by victim statements where victims appear to be submissive during the perpetration of the acts due to fear for their personal safety or to the fear of upsetting adults. This finding is increasingly supported by large victim surveys (Roberts, 1993; Maker et al., 1998; Cawson, 2000).

Attempts to discover the true incidence of abuse in the UK have been few. The most notable studies include Mrazek, Lynch and Bentovim's (1981) early survey of general practitioners, paediatricians, child psychiatrists and police surgeons, all of whom were asked for information (anonymously) regarding children seen between June 1977 and May 1978 who were believed to be have been sexually abused. The response rate was low (39 per cent), and this may in part be attributable to professional–patient confidentiality. However, some 1,072 cases were reported as being seen during the specified time period. On this basis Mrazek et al. suggested that approximately 1 in 6,000 children are affected, a very low estimate compared to the findings of other studies. The validity of this work may be questioned, given the low response rate and the possibility of non-response bias. Nash and West (1985), in their study of adult women registered with GPs and female students, found rates of 42 per cent for the GP sample and 53 per cent for the student sample: very few of the offences had been reported to the police. The operational definition was, however, broad, including abuse involving no physical contact such as obscene suggestions and the showing of pornographic material.

Statistics produced by the Department for Education and Skills (DfES) in England shed little light on the extent of the problem, indicating that there were 2,600 children and young people on child protection registers for sexual abuse in 2006 (representing 8 per cent of the total number of children and young people on registers). The figures suggest a decrease in this category from 4,500 (17 per cent) in 2001 (Figure 1.5), which is difficult to account for (DfES, 2006) but could in part be attributable to the creation of a 'mixed abuse' category in 2002; this data provides a somewhat misleading picture.

Kelly et al.'s (1991) British research confirms Nash and West's findings: over 1,000 students were surveyed; a rate of 59 per cent

2001 N(%)	2002 N(%)	2003 N(%)	2004 N(%)	2005 N(%)	2006 N(%)
4,500(17)	2,800(11)	2,700(10)	2,500(9)	2,400(9)	2,600(8)

Figure 1.5 Number and proportion of children and young people on child protection registers in England at 31 March 2001–2006 – sexual abuse
Source: DfES 2006

was reported among females compared to 27 per cent among males (child sexual abuse was defined as at least one unwanted sexual experience involving some physical contact prior to age 18, ranging from touching to full penetration).

The findings from large-scale surveys tend to be inconsistent and are dependent upon the definition of abuse adopted. Research was conducted by the NSPCC in 1997 using a broad definition of sexual abuse. The findings suggested that 1 in 7 of the population had experienced sexual abuse as a child. It is worth noting that those studies reporting higher rates of abuse have the highest survey response rates, although not necessarily the largest samples, and many employed interview techniques. The high variation in incidence rates reported both by British and North American research is certainly due to different definitions of child sexual abuse adopted, but also, at least in part, to varying research methodologies. Cawson et al.'s (2000) more recent work on behalf of the NSPCC suggests that 16 per cent of children and young people under 16 experienced sexual abuse as a child (Figure 1.6).

More recent research conducted by May-Chahal and Cawson (2005) has sought to explore the incidence of child abuse in the UK. The findings suggest that 16 per cent of the 2,869 sample of young adults reported experiencing some form of abuse. The authors conclude that child abuse remains an extensive problem in the UK.

- One per cent of under 16s were sexually abused by a parent or carer

- Three per cent were sexually abused by a relative

- Brothers and step-brothers were most commonly the perpetrator of sexually abusive acts in intra-familial abuse (38 per cent). In 23 per cent of cases fathers were the perpetrator.

- Eleven per cent were sexually abused by a person known to them but unrelated

- Five per cent were sexually abused by a stranger

- Eleven per cent of boys and 21 per cent of girls were sexually abused as children

- The majority of children and young people who were sexually abused were abused on more than one occasion

Figure 1.6 Key findings of Cawson's study
Source: Cawson et al., NSPCC, 2000, pp 83–6

Prevalence in cyberspace

Recent research indicates that sex offenders use the internet to target and 'groom' children for the purposes of sexual abuse (Wolak and Finkelhor, 2000); to produce and/or download indecent illegal images of children for distribution; and to communicate with other sex offenders (Quayle and Taylor, 2002; Davidson, 2007). Gillan (2003) has suggested that the demand for indecent images through, for example, the use of file-sharing technologies, has expanded so much that law enforcement agencies are finding it increasingly difficult to identify and track down child victims and the perpetrators involved (Gillan, 2003; Davidson, 2007).

Many child victims appearing in indecent images are among the most vulnerable, from poor countries, and are repeat victims. The police are attempting to identify victims from the images produced on the internet but the process is slow and time-consuming, and yields little identification (Davidson, 2007). The IWF have reported a rise in the number of websites containing indecent images of children from 3,438 in 2004 to 6,000 in 2006. The websites are hosted outside of the UK, and are therefore extremely difficult to police and control.

There is no doubt that such abuse has a damaging and negative impact upon child victims. It has been claimed that in many instances children are abused and the abuse recorded by members of their own family or people known to them (Klain et al., 2001). Many indecent images depict the sexual abuse of children who are victimised both in the creation of the image and in the distribution of the image. It could be argued that a child is re-victimised each time their image is accessed, and images on the internet can form a permanent record of abuse.

Key chapter themes

- The concept of 'childhood' has changed over time. Attempts to afford children and young people greater protection and access to justice have not been entirely successful and adolescent 'hoodies' are portrayed by the media as a threat to the social order.

- The age of informed consent to sexual relations could be taken to be indicative of social attitudes towards the transition from 'childhood' to 'adulthood'. In the UK the age of consent was once as low as 10, it is now set at 16.

• Recent legislation (the Sexual Offences Act 2003 – England and Wales) has introduced a new offence category 'grooming' and now seeks to control abuse in cyberspace. Informed consent is now not an issue to be debated in sexual abuse cases involving children under 13.

• Official estimates of the sexual abuse of children do not accurately reflect the extent of the problem – victims' surveys and victim accounts suggest that such abuse occurs on a wider scale and is largely unreported. Such research also demonstrates that victims frequently suffer trauma as a consequence of childhood abuse into adult life.

References

Allen, R, 'From punishment to problem solving – a new approach to children in trouble', accessed 12 June 2006, www.kcl.ac.uk/depsta/rel/ccjs/2006-punishment-to-problem-solving.html

Aries, P, *Centuries of Childhood: A Social History of Family Life*, 1962, New York: Vintage Books

Ashworth, A, *Principles of Criminal Law*, 3rd edn, 1999, New York: Oxford University Press

Autograph Letter Collection: *Letters Related To William Thomas Stead 1885–1924*, The Women's Library, www.londonmet.ac.uk/thewomenslibrary/aboutthecollections/archive/archive-collections/strand-9-autograph-letter-collection.cfm

Baker, A and Duncan, S, 'Child sexual abuse: A study of prevalence in Great Britain', *Child Abuse and Neglect*, 9 (1985), pp 457–67

Beech, A, Fisher, D, Beckett, R and Fordham, A S, 'STEP 3: An evaluation of the prison sex offender treatment programme', 1998, Home Office Research, Development and Statistics Occasional Paper, London: Home Office

Benjamin, A, 'Welcome surprise of a successful ASBO', *Guardian*, 20 December 2006

Bequele, A, 'Ideals without illusions: Promoting child rights in the context of poverty', key note address delivered at the XVII ISPCAN International Congress on Child Abuse and Neglect, 'Children in a changing world: Getting it right', 3–6 September 2006, York, UK

Blackman, O, 'Fifty per cent of ASBOs broken', *Daily Mirror*, 7 December 2006

Briere, J and Runtz, M, 'Suicidal thoughts and behaviour in sexual abuse survivors', *Canadian Journal of Behavioural Sciences*, 18 (1986), pp 413–23

Briere, J and Runtz, M, 'Symptomology associated with childhood sexual victimization in a nonclinical adult sample', *Child Abuse and Neglect*, 12 (1988), pp 51–9

British Fashion Council, 'Model health inquiry', Press Release, 23 March 2007

Brown, L and Holder, W, 'The nature and extent of child abuse in contemporary American society', in Holder, W (ed), *Sexual Abuse of Children*, 1980, Colorado: AHA

Canter, D and Alison, L, *Profiling in Policy and Practice*, 1999, Dartmouth: Ashgate

Carter, B J, *Who's to Blame? Child Sexual Abuse and Non-offending Mothers*, 1999, Toronto: University of Toronto Press

Cawson, P, Wattam, S and Kelly, G, *Child Maltreatment in the UK: A Study of the Prevalence of Child Abuse and Neglect*, 2000, London: NSPCC

Chauhan, C, 'Law ministry rejects bill for child protection', *Hindustan Times*, 4 September 2007, accessed November 2007, www.hindustantimes. com/storypage/storypage.aspx?id=2cef17ef-f024-474c-9051-112c525 be97b&&Headline=Ministry+rejects+bill+for+child+protection

Chen, J Q, Dunne, M and Han, P, 'Child sexual abuse in China: A study of adolescents in four provinces', *Child Abuse and Neglect*, 28(11) (2004), pp 1171–86

Child Exploitation and Online Protection Centre (CEOP), 2006, accessed December 2006, www.ceop.gov.uk

Clarke, G, 'They measured my fingers to see if I was fat', *Daily Mail*, 29 May 2007

Cobley, C, *Child Abuse and the Law*, 1995, London: Cavendish

Coveney, P, 'The image of the child', in Jenks, C (ed), *The Sociology of Childhood*, 1982, London: Batsford Academic

Creighton, C, *Prevalence and Incidence of Child Abuse: International Comparisons*, 2004, London: NSPCC

Davidson, J, 'The context and practice of community treatment programmes for convicted child sexual abusers in England and Wales', unpublished PhD thesis, 2001, London School of Economics and Political Science

Davidson, J, 'Child sexual abuse prevention programmes: The role of schools', in Giotakos, O, Eher, R and Pfäfflin, F (eds), *Sex Offending is Everybody's Business*, 8th International Conference of the International Association for the Treatment of Sexual Offenders, 6–9 October 2004, Pabst: Lengerich

Davidson, J, 'Victims speak: Comparing child sexual abusers and child victims accounts, perceptions and interpretations of sexual abuse', *Victims and Offenders*, 1(2) (2006), pp 159–74

Davidson, J, 'Current practice and research into internet sex offending', 2007, www.rmascotland.gov.uk/ViewFile.aspx?id=235, Risk Management Authority (Scotland)

Davidson, J and Martellozzo, E, 'Educating children about sexual abuse and evaluating the Metropolitan Police Safer Surfing Programme', 2004, accessed 5 June 2007, www.saferschoolpartnerships.org/ssp-topics/evaluations/documents/ssfindingsreport.pdf

Davidson, J and Martellozzo, E, 'Policing the internet and protecting children from sex offenders online: When strangers become "virtual friends"', paper given at Cybersafety Conference, University of Oxford, 8–10 September 2005, accessed December 2006, www.oii.ox.ac.uk/microsites/cybersafety/?view=papers

Davidson, J, Bifulco, A, Thomas, G and Ramsey, M, 'Child victims of sexual abuse: Children's experience of the investigative process in the criminal justice system', *Practice Journal*, 18 (2006) pp 267–74

Davis, G, 'The admissability and sufficiency of evidence in child abuse prosecutions', 1999, Research Findings No 100: Home Office

Deb, S and Sen, P, 'A study on psychological trauma of young trafficked women', in Daro, D (ed), *World Perspectives on Child Abuse*, 7th edn, 2006, ISPCAN (International Society for Prevention of Child Abuse and Neglect)

DeMause, L, 'The evolution of childhood', in Jenks, C (ed), *The Sociology of Childhood*, 1982, London: Batsford Academic

Department for Education and Skills, 'Referrals, assessments and children and young people on child protection registers, England. Year ending 31 March 2006', 2006, accessed 3 December 2006, www.dfes.gov.uk/rsgateway/DB/SFR/s000692/SFR45-2006V1.pdf

DeYoung, M, *Sexual Victimisation of Children*, 1982, New York: McFarland

Doyle-Peters, S, 'Child sexual abuse and later psychological problems', in Wyatt, G, and Powell, G (eds), *Lasting Effects of Child Sexual Abuse*, 1988, London: Sage

Dunne, M P, and MacFarlane, B, 'Improving instruments for international research into child abuse', in Daro, D (ed), *World Perspectives on Child Abuse*, 7th edn, 2006, ISPCAN

ECPAT, New Zealand, 'End child prostitution, child pornography and trafficking children for sexual purposes', accessed 3 December 2006, www.ecpat.org.nz/projects-research.html

Finkelhor, D, *Child Sexual Abuse: New Theory and Research*, 1984, New York: Free Press

Finkelhor, D, *Four conditions: A Model of Child Sexual Abuse: New Theories and Research*, 1986, New York: Free Press

Finkelhor, D, Araji, S, Baron, L, Browne, A, Doyle-Peters, S and Wyatt, G E, *A Sourcebook on Child Sexual Abuse*, 1986, California: Sage

Fisher, D, 'Sex offenders: Who are they, why are they?', in Morrison, T, Erooga, M and Beckett, R (eds), *Sexual Offending Against Children: Assessment and Treatment of Male Abusers*, 1994, London: Routledge

Fitch, J H, 'Men convicted of sexual offences against children: A follow up study', *British Journal of Criminology*, 3(1) (1962), pp 18–37

Fordham, A S, 'Evaluating sex offender treatment programmes', paper given at the British Psychological Society Conference, 1992, Bath

Foreign and Commonwealth Office, 'Child rights 2005', accessed November 2006, www.fco.gov.uk/servlet/Front?Pagename=OpenMarket/Xcelerate/ShowPage&c=Pag&cid=1028302591869

Fraser, B G, 'Sexual child abuse: Legislation and law in the US', in Mrazek, P B and Kempe, C (eds), *Sexually Abused Children and their Families*, 1981, Oxford: Pergamon

Fromouth, M E, 'The long-term psychological impact of childhood sexual abuse', unpublished paper, 1983

Galvin, M (British Telecom Director of Internet Safety) 'A responsibility shared: Finding solutions to protect children online', presentation at Institute for Public Policy Research, 2 November 2004, www.ippr.org.uk/research/teams/event.asp?id=1048&pID=0&tID=95

Gillan, A, 'Race to save new victims of child pornography', *Guardian*, 4 November 2003

Grubin, D, ' Sex offending against children understanding the risk', *Home Office Police Research Series*, 99, Webb, B (ed), 1998, accessed January 2007, www.homeoffice.gov.uk/rds/prgpdfs/fprs99.pdf

Gudjonsson, G, 'The revised Gudjonsson blame attribution inventory', *Personal Individual Differences*, 10(1) (1987), pp 67–70

Gudjonsson, G, 'Self-deception and other deception in forensic assessment', *Personal Individual Differences*, 11(3) (1990), pp 219–25

Harris, J and Grace, S, 'A question of evidence? Investigating and prosecuting rape in the 1990s', 1999, Home Office Research Study 196

Herman, J L, 'Sex offenders: A feminist perspective', in Marshall, W L, Laws, D R and Barbaree, H E, *Handbook of Sexual Assault: Issues, Theories and Treatment of the Offender*, 1991, New York: Plenu

Holder, W, *Sexual Abuse of Children*, 1980, Colorado: AHA

Home Office, 'Protecting the public: Strengthening protection against sex offenders and reforming the law on sexual offences', 2002, London: Home Office

Home Office, 'Explanatory notes to Sexual Offences Act 2003', Home Office, 2003, accessed 17 May 2006, www.homeoffice.gov.uk/crime/antisocialbehaviour/orders/

Home Office Crime Statistics for England and Wales, 2006, accessed 4 December 2006, www.homeoffice.gov.uk/CrimeStatisticsforEngland andWales-Long-termnationalrecordedcrimetrendSexualoffences.htm

Home Office Task Force on Child Protection on the Internet, 'Good practice models and guidance for the internet industry on: chat services; instant messages; web based services', accessed 10 November 2007, http://police.homeoffice.gov.uk/news-and-publications/publication/operational-policing/ho_model.pdf?view=Binary

'Hoodies broke woman's hip . . .' Daily Mail, 30 January 2007

Howard League, 'Unlawful sex', report of a Howard League working party, 1985, London: Waterlow

Howells, K, 'Some meanings of children for paedophiles', in Cook, M and Wilson, F (eds), Love and Attraction, 1979, London: Pergamon

Institute for Public Policy Research Conference, 'Manifesto for a digital Britain: A responsibility shared? Finding solutions to protect children online', accessed 10 November 2007, www.ippr.org.uk/research/teams/event.asp?id=1048&pID=0&tID=95

Internet Watch Foundation, 'Remove online images of child abuse', Press Release and Conference, 24 October 2006

Jenks, C (ed), The Sociology of Childhood, 1982, London: Batsford Academics

Jenks, C, Childhood, 1996, London: Routledge

Jensen, T K, Gulbrandson, W, Mossige, S, Reichelt, S and Tjersland, O A, 'Reporting possible sexual abuse: A qualitative study on children's perspectives and the context for disclosure', Child Abuse and Neglect, 29 (2005), pp 1395–413

Kelly, J, ' Is the MySpace net closing in?', BBC News Online, 19 January 2007, http://news.bbc.co.uk/1/hi/uk/6275611.stm

Kelly, L, Surviving Sexual Violence, 1988, Oxford: Blackwell

Kelly, L, Lovett, J and Regan, L, 'A gap or chasm? Attrition in reported rape cases', 2005, Home Office Research Study 293, London: HMSO

Kelly, L, Regan, L and Burton, S, 'An exploratory study of the prevalence of sexual abuse in a sample of 16–31 year olds', 1991, North London University, Child Abuse Studies Unit. London: PNL

Kercher, G and McShane, M, 'The prevalence of child sexual abuse victimization in an adult sample of Texas residents', Child Abuse and Neglect, 8 (1984), pp 495–502

Klain, E J, Davis, H J and Hicks, M A, 'Child pornography: The criminal justice service response', American Bar Association Centre on Children and the Law for the National Center for Missing and Exploited Children, 2001, accessed January 2007, www.popcenter.org/Problems/Supplemental_Material/childpornography/Klain_etal_2001.pdf

Kvam, M H, 'Sexual abuse of deaf children: A retrospective analysis of the prevalence and characteristics of childhood sexual abuse amongst deaf adults in Norway', Child Abuse and Neglect, 28(3) (2004), pp 241–51

La Fontaine, J, 'Child sexual abuse', 1988, an ESRC Research Briefing, London: ERSC

Maker, A H, Kemmelmeier, M and Peterson, C, 'Long term psychological consequences in women of witnessing parental physical conflict and experiencing abuse in childhood', *Journal Interpersonal Violence*, 13(5) (1998), pp 575–89

Marshall, W L, 'The relationship between self esteem and deviant sexual arousal in non-familial child sexual molesters', *Behaviour Modification*, 21 (1997), pp 86–96

Martin, G, Bergen, H, Richardson, A, Roeger, L and Allison, S, 'Sexual abuse and suicidality: Gender differences in a large community sample of adolescents', *Child Abuse and Neglect*, 28(5) (2004), pp 491–503

May-Chahal, C and Cawson, P, 'Measuring child maltreatment in the UK: A study of the prevalence of child abuse and neglect', *Child Abuse and Neglect*, 29(9) (2005), pp 969–84

Miles, G, 'Stop violence against us: Cambodian children's perceptions of violence' in Daro, D (ed.), *World Perspectives on Child Abuse*, 7th edn, 2006, ISPCAN

Mitra, K and Deb, S, 'Socio-economic profile and cognitive ability of street children', in Daro, D (ed.), *World Perspectives on Child Abuse*, 7th edn, 2006, ISPCAN

MORI, 'Survey of child sexual abuse', MORI (1984), p 2548

MORI, 'Survey of child sexual abuse', MORI (1988), p 3942

Morris, I, Scott, I, Mortimer, R and Barker, D, 'Physical and sexual abuse of children in the West Midlands', *Child Abuse and Neglect*, 21(3) (1997), pp 285–93

Morrison, T, Erooga, M and Beckett, R, *Sexual Offending Against Children*, 1994, London: Routledge

Mrazek, P B and Kemp, C H, *Sexually Abused Children and Their Families*, 1981, Oxford: Pergamon Press

Mrazek, P B, Lynch, M and Bentovim, A, 'Recognition of child sexual abuse in the United Kingdom', in Mrazek, P B and Kempe, C H, *Sexually Abused Children and their Families*, 1981, Oxford: Pergamon Press

Nash, C L and West, D J, 'Sexual molestation of young girls: A retrospective study', in West, D J (ed), *Sexual Victimisation*, 1985, Aldershot: Gower

Nava, M, 'Cleveland and the press: Outrage and anxiety in the reporting of child sexual abuse', *Feminist Review*, 28 (1988), pp 103–21

Neate, P, *Child Abuse: Scare in the Community, Britain in a Moral Panic*, 1995, Reed Business Publishing: London

Neumann, D, 'The long term sequelae of childhood sexual abuse in women: A meta analytical review', *Child Maltreatment*, 1(1) (1996), pp 17–24

Peters, J J, 'Children who are the victims of sexual assault and the psychology of offenders', *American Journal of Psychotherapy*, 3 (1976), pp 395–421

Peters, S D, 'The relationship between childhood sexual victimisation and depression amongst Afro-American and white women', in Wyatt, G, and Powell, G, *Lasting Effects of Child Sexual Abuse*, 1984, London: Sage

Plotnikoff, J and Woolfson, R, 'In their own words: The experiences of 50 young witnesses in criminal proceedings', 2004, London: NSPCC

Prince, R, 'We fear our teens, Britons too scared . . .' *Daily Mirror*, 23 October 2006

Quayle, E and Taylor, M, 'Child seduction and self-representation on the internet', *Cyberpsychology and Behaviour*, 4(5) (2001), pp 597–607

Quayle, E and Taylor, M, 'Paedophiles, pornography and the internet: Assessment issues', *British Journal of Social Work*, 32 (2002), pp 863–75

Quayle, E and Taylor, M, 'Model of problematic internet use in people with a sexual interest in children', *Cyberpsychology and Behaviour*, 6(1) (2003), pp 93–106

Roberts, J, 'Sexually abused children and young people speak out', in Waterhouse, L, *Child Abuse and Child Abusers*, 1993, California: Sage

Romans, S and Martin, J, 'Childhood sexual abuse and later psychological problems: Neither necessary, sufficient nor acting alone', *Criminal Behaviour and Mental Health*, 7 (1997), pp 327–8

Roth-Szamoskozi, M (2000), 'Child welfare in Romania', *Studia Universitatis Babes-Bolyai – Sociology*, 2 (2006), pp 95–121

Russell, D, 'The incidence and prevalence of intra-familial and extra-familial sexual abuse of female children', *Child Abuse and Neglect*, 7 (1983), pp 133–46

Russell, D, *The Secret Trauma: Incest in the Lives of Girls and Women*, 1984, New York: Basil Books

Salter, A, *Treating Child Sex Offenders and Victims: A Practical Guide*, 1988, California: Sage

Sampson, A, *Acts of Abuse: Sex Offenders and the Criminal Justice System*, 1994, London: Routledge

Scully, D, *Understanding Sexual Violence: A Study of Convicted Rapists*, 1990, Boston: Unwin Heinemann

Sexual Offences Act 2003, Home Office website, accessed February 2007, www.homeoffice.gov.uk/documents/adults-safe-fr-sex-harm-leafet?version=1

Summit, R C, 'Hidden victims, hidden pain', in Wyatt, G and Powell, G, *Lasting Effects of Child Sexual Abuse*, 1988, California: Sage

Thompson, E P, *The Making of the English Working Class*, 1982, London: Penguin Books

Van Niekirk, J (National Coordinator, Childline, South Africa), 2007, email correspondence

Waterhouse, L, *Child Abuse and Child Abusers*, 1983, California: Sage

Waterhouse, R, 'Lost in care: Report of the Tribunal of Inquiry into the abuse of children in care in the former county council areas of Gwynedd and Clwyd since 1974', 2000, accessed 10 November 2007, www.dh.gov.uk/en/Publicationsandstatistics/Publications/PublicationsPolicyAndGuidance/Browsable/DH_4928354

Wolak, J and Finkelhor, D, 'First youth internet safety survey – Y1SS-1', 2000, University of New Hampshire, www.unh.edu/ccrc/youth_internet_safety_survey.html

Woods, V, 'Britons have never liked children', *Daily Telegraph*, 4 January 2006

Wright, R, 'Rape and physical violence', in West, D J (ed), *Sex Offenders in the Criminal Justice System*, 1984, Cambridge: Cambridge Institute of Criminology

Wyatt, G, and Powell, G, *Lasting Effects of Child Sexual Abuse*, 1988, New York: Sage

Ystgaard, M, Hestetun, I, Loeb, M and Mehlum, L, 'Is there a specific relationship between childhood sexual abuse and physical abuse and suicidal behaviour?', *Child Abuse and Neglect*, 28(8) (2004), pp 863–75

Chapter 2

The crisis in child protection and child victims' access to justice

This chapter seeks to:

- Explore the impact of key child abuse investigations upon government policy.

- Explore media representations of such investigations and consider the impact upon agencies concerned with child protection.

- Consider why few cases involving the sexual abuse of children are prosecuted.

The Cleveland, Rochdale and Orkney Inquiries

The realisation that child sexual abuse is a serious social problem, the extent of which is probably greater than had been previously thought, was brought about during the late 1980s and early 1990s. First, revelations regarding large-scale intra-familial sexual abuse of children in Cleveland in 1986 appeared to confirm the suspicions of welfare workers that children were suffering sexual abuse in their own families, while the ensuing media coverage served to fuel public anxiety. Second, large-scale victim surveys conducted by feminists such as Kelly (1988) began to suggest that a considerable proportion of adults had experienced sexual abuse as a child within their own families. The 1980s also saw a turning point in government attitudes towards the family as an institution that should be largely self-regulating and free from interference. Saraga (1998) suggests that this accompanied a shift in attitude towards welfare intervention, from the provision of therapeutic family work to a focus upon removal of the perpetrator from the family and criminal investigation. This has been accompanied by a further shift towards focus upon the effective risk management of serious violent and sexual offenders (this is explored further in Chapter Five).

The Cleveland case involved 121 children who were forcibly removed from their families on suspicion of being sexually abused. When the accusations made against the children's families proved to be unfounded, a public inquiry was set up, chaired by Dame Elisabeth Butler-Sloss. The Butler-Sloss Report (1988) criticised the manner in which doctors and social workers identified sexual abuse on the basis of inconclusive evidence. The Cleveland case added another dimension to increasing public anxiety regarding child abuse, for not only were children at risk, but social workers were clearly incapable of successfully identifying abuse. Cleveland triggered a crisis in public confidence regarding the social work profession and child protection that was exacerbated by subsequent similar cases.

In the wake of the Cleveland Inquiry the Conservative Government responded to public concern regarding the protection and standing of children with the publication of the 1989 Children Act. This act sought to impress upon professionals concerned with child welfare the importance of working in the best interests of the child when involved in child protection work. The legislation also sought to afford children (aged seven and over) some control over their lives, by instructing professionals involved in child protection and civil work to take the child's view into account in making decisions concerning their future and well being.

Shortly after the Cleveland case allegations of satanic child abuse arose in Rochdale and Orkney. In 1989, in Rochdale, Lancashire, children were forcibly removed from their homes in police raids and placed in the care of social services following allegations that their parents were actively involved in a satanic abuse network. No convictions ensued due to lack of evidence, but despite this some of the children remained in care, having little contact with their parents. One child removed at the age of 6 was held in care until the age of 16 (*The Times* online, 2006). In 1991 further allegations of satanic abuse led to the removal of children by the police from their families in the Orkney Islands. When the case came to court it was dismissed by the presiding judge, Sheriff David Kelbie, due to insufficient evidence. Sheriff Kelbie publicly criticised the social workers, police and doctors for making unfounded allegations, claiming that their case was 'fundamentally flawed'. He suggested that interviewing techniques employed by professionals had led the children to respond positively to allegations. If the public had forgotten recent similar cases, the judge reminded them when he stated that social workers had learnt little from Cleveland and Rochdale. The media responded swiftly; the BBC declared 'Orkney "abuse" children go home' (4 April 1991). The lasting effects of these cases are still very much apparent: the *Scotsman* has claimed that a woman involved in the Orkney case who was removed from her family and placed in the care of social services for six years is planning to sue the council, seeking damages to the sum of £100, 000 for 'lost childhood' (*Scotsman*, 2006).

It has been claimed that a 'moral panic' regarding the incidence and nature of child abuse has developed as a consequence of such inquiries. This panic has been fuelled by media attention and public anxiety, culminating in a lack of confidence among child welfare professionals and an inability to 'get on with the job' (Neate, 1995, p 30). Cohen (2002) has suggested that each moral panic produces its own demons and moral scapegoats. Child abusers continue to be demonised by the media and Neate (1995) suggests that social workers involved in child protection work represent the scapegoats in this particular panic. Moral panics have been described in largely negative terms as representing misplaced social anxiety regarding a group of people and the threat they pose (Hall et al., 1978). In the case of child sexual abuse, such anxiety may not be misplaced. Although unsubstantiated, cases such as Cleveland and Orkney may have forced society to acknowledge the possibility that children have been, and continue to be, sexually abused on a scale never before imagined, and frequently within the family and by trusted friends. In the search for monsters and scapegoats it is possible to forget that the sexual abuse of children should be the primary cause for concern. The nature of this particular moral panic may obscure reality, but social indifference regarding the issue would be far worse.

The Waterhouse Inquiry

The publication of a report entitled *Lost in Care* written by former High Court Judge Sir Ronald Waterhouse (February 2000) can have done little to restore public confidence in child care professionals.[1] The report indicated that up to 650 children were sexually and physically abused over two decades in children's homes in North Wales. The fallout from Cleveland, Rochdale and Orkney may have suggested that care professionals could not competently recognise child sexual abuse, but Waterhouse suggested that some of those professionals charged with the care of vulnerable children and young adults were in reality predatory sexual abusers. Subsequently 25 social workers have received custodial sentences for child sexual abuse in North Wales children's homes. The situation was exacerbated by revelations regarding the abuse of children in other care homes.

The aims of the Waterhouse Inquiry (2000) were fourfold: to explore the abuse of children in care in the former county councils of Gwynedd and Clwyd since 1974; to examine to what extent the responsible agencies could have prevented the abuse; to examine the response of the agencies; and to consider if appropriate action was taken. The inquiry concluded that widespread sexual abuse of children (mainly boys) occurred in local authority homes, private children's homes and some foster homes in the area between 1974 and 1990. The authors also suggested that the scale of the abuse was under-reported given their inability to investigate further. The authors criticised practice and the quality of care provided at every level. Such criticism included the absence of a complaints procedure and an unwillingness to listen to children's accounts of abuse; the manner in which staff were recruited without police checks; inadequate staff training opportunities; infrequent visiting by field social workers; and inadequate recording of events. The authors describe a situation in which organisational inadequacies within social services and at local level gave rise to circumstances in which it was possible for abusers to gain employment as care workers and sexually abuse children over a long period of time. The authors recommendations were in keeping with the Children Act 1989 in stressing that action should always be taken in the best interests of the child.

---

1   The Tribunal of Inquiry into Child Abuse in North Wales was ordered by both Houses of Parliament in 1996. Sir Ronald Waterhouse, Margaret Clough and Morris Le Fleming were appointed by William Hague, then the Secretary of State for Wales, to undertake the inquiry.

- The appointment of an Independent Children's Commissioner

- The appointment of a Children's Complaints Officer by every social services authority, who would respond to every child complaint

- The establishment of clear whistle-blowing procedures

- Failure by staff to report suspected abuse of a child by anyone else should become a disciplinary offence

- An individual social worker should be allocated to every child in care, who must be visited by them every eight weeks

Figure 2.1 Waterhouse Report key recommendations
Source: The Waterhouse Report, 2000

The media wasted no time in bringing the key findings of the Waterhouse Report to the public's attention, focusing on the plight of the victims and the incompetence of a system which allowed the abuse to continue for 20 years.

The *Sun* devoted half of its front page to the story with the headline 'I Nailed Child Sex Perverts', and a story about Alison Taylor, who first made the claim. Inside the paper the plight of the victims was considered, with headlines such as 'The Lost Children Suffered 20 Years of Abuse' and 'Monsters Stole my Childhood' (*Sun*, 10 October 2000). The *Daily Telegraph* was highly critical of the agencies involved in the Climbie case: 'The People who Failed Victoria' suggested one headline and the paper went on to comment upon the 'incompetence, blindness and stupidity of the officials who were supposed to be protecting Victoria' (*Daily Telegraph*, 9 October 2001). The paper criticised the ability of local authorities to care adequately and appropriately for children. The *Guardian* newspaper covered the story extensively, providing a brief summary of the 72 recommendations made by the Waterhouse Report, suggesting that management of the social care system was inadequate (*Guardian*, 11 October 2000). *The Times* headlined with 'Youngsters in Care still at Risk, says Abuse Report' (*The Times*, 11 October 2000). The story focused upon the victims and gave a full account of the parliamentary debate, demanding action as a consequence of the report: 'Waterhouse's report must not join its predecessors on the shelf.'

The Waterhouse Report also drew attention to the position of young people in care aged 16–17 who may be uncertain about their sexuality and who were vulnerable to sexual abuse by predatory adults but not protected in law:

> We have concentrated our attention on evidence relating to children who were in care at the time, having regard to our terms of reference, but we have necessarily heard some evidence about others who were on the fringe of the care system, that is, children who were later committed to care and youths who had recently been discharged from care. In our judgment, the perils for such persons are as great in this respect as for those actually in care and our findings emphasise the importance of continuing support by social services for those who are discharged from care.

A specific case is discussed by way of example:

> We draw the attention of Parliament also to the abuse suffered by B between the ages of 16 years and 18 years, in circumstances which appear to have made him question his own sexuality for a period. Much of the later abuse was not inflicted by persons in a position of trust in relation to him and there can be no doubt that he was significantly corrupted and damaged by what occurred.
>
> (Waterhouse, 2000, para 52.87)

The Waterhouse Report drew attention to several types of sexual abuse that had been experienced by the children (now adults) giving evidence:

- 'Grooming': socialising and preparing a young person for abuse on leaving the home;
- 'Farming out': children from one home abused by care staff from another home;
- Absconders: children who cease to be 'resident' but are abused by the care staff from the home;
- Abuse by ancillary staff;
- Abuse by a social services inspector;
- Abuse in youth organisations.

Just as the Cleveland affair became a watershed in child protection work, simultaneously raising the public consciousness via the media regarding the incidence of abuse and criticising professionals for the use of inadequate abuse identification techniques, the Waterhouse Report constituted a second watershed: media reporting that served to refocus public attention upon these issues and underlined the view that those professionals who are entrusted with the care of children and young people are well placed to sexually abuse them.

The Laming Inquiry

The third and probably most significant watershed in child protection work involved the physical abuse (and probable sexual abuse) and murder of a child known to several social services departments, local authorities and hospital casualty departments, and on the 'at risk' register at the time of her death. Victoria Climbie was born in the Ivory Coast on 2 November 1991 and travelled to London to start a new life with her aunt in 1999. Following numerous trips to the Casualty Department at the North Middlesex Hospital, Victoria died in the Intensive Care Unit of St Mary's Hospital, London, with 128 separate injuries (Victoria Climbie Inquiry, 2003).

In April 2001 Lord Laming was appointed to conduct three independent statutory inquiries, under the Children Act 1989, the National Health Act 1977 and the Police Act 1996, into the death of Victoria Climbie. The inquiry aimed to explore how agencies had discharged their duties to Victoria before her death, and to make recommendations regarding how safeguards for children might be strengthened in future. The physical abuse endured by Victoria was horrendous and sustained, leading Laming to comment:

> at the end Victoria spent the cold winter months, bound hand and foot, in an unheated bathroom, lying in the cold bath in a plastic bag in her own urine and faeces and having to eat what food she could get by pressing her face onto the plate of whatever was put in the bath beside her. Little wonder that at the time of her last admission to hospital her body temperature was so low it did not register on a standard thermometer and her legs could not be straightened. So in a few months this once lively, bright and energetic child had been reduced to a bruised, deformed and malnourished state in which her life ebbed away because of the total collapse of her body systems.

(Laming, 2003, p 3)

14 July 1999 – Victoria attends Casualty at Central Middlesex Hospital with suspected non-accidental injuries. She is released back into her aunt's care and diagnosed with scabies.

24 July 1999 – Victoria attends North Middlesex Hospital with suspected non-accidental injuries (scalding to neck and face).

6 August 1999 – Victoria released back into the care of her aunt (Kouao) after two weeks in North Middlesex Hospital.

1 November 1999 – Kouao claims that her boyfriend (Manning) had sexually abused Victoria. The claim was withdrawn the following day.

24 February 2000 – Victoria admitted to Casualty at North Middlesex Hospital and is then transferred to St Mary's hospital.

25 February 2000 – Victoria pronounced dead at 3.15pm with 128 separate non-accidental injuries.

12 January 2001 – Marie Thérèse Kouao and Carl Manning are given life sentences for Victoria's murder. The Health Secretary orders a statutory inquiry into her death led by Lord Laming. Haringey Social Services department placed under special measures requiring close supervision by the social services inspectorate.

Figure 2.2 Victoria Climbie time line – key events
Source: Laming (2003)

The Climbie case revealed an astonishing degree of incompetence on the part of agencies concerned, including social services, the local authority, medical staff and the police. The key events are described in Figure 2.2.

The Laming Inquiry pointed to the number of occasions on which Victoria's plight might have been noted and acted upon by the agencies concerned, as the most basic interventions were absent in this case. The agencies were all aware of Victoria's existence from an early point, indeed Laming states:

Nor was Victoria hidden from view such that great time or resources would have been necessary in order to discover her needs. On the second day she and Kouao were in this country Kouao and Victoria visited the homeless persons unit in the London Borough of Ealing. In the months which followed Victoria was known to no fewer than four social services departments, three housing departments, two specialist child protection teams of the Metropolitan Police. Furthermore, she was admitted to two different hospitals because of concerns that she was being deliberately harmed and was referred to a specialist children and families centre managed by the NSPCC. All of this between 26th April 1999 and 25th February 2000.

(Laming, 2003, p 2)

Laming attributed the death of Victoria Climbie to professional, administrative and managerial failings in the care system. The media agreed and launched a sustained campaign against the professionals Laming had criticised: the *Daily Mail* stated 'Climbie Child Protection "Disgrace"' (7 November 2001). The newspaper went on to criticise the key social worker who failed to attend the Laming Inquiry (3 December 2001). It could be argued that the social worker did nothing to restore public confidence in the profession by failing to attend the inquiry until forced to do so. The *Sun* appeared to devote a less sustained onslaught against the agencies involved in the Climbie case than the *Daily Mail*, with headlines such as 'Disgrace of the Bosses who let Victoria Die' (29 January 2003) and 'Victoria File was Altered' (*Sun*, 23 November 2001), referring to the suggestion that a social worker altered key documentation following Victoria's death to cover up mistakes. The *Guardian* newspaper had a great deal more to say regarding the behaviour of the agencies involved, criticising the police child protection officer in uncharacteristic tabloid style claiming that the police officer investigating the case failed to visit fearing scabies (*Guardian*, 19 November 2001) and commenting on the under-resourcing of the social services departments involved (*Guardian*, 18 October 2001). The newspaper blamed the incompetence and disorganisation of social services for Victoria's death and the inexperience of the key social worker who it is claimed was not properly managed (*Guardian*, 28 September 2001 and 5 October 2001).

Lord Laming made several key recommendations (Figure 2.3), some of which have been implemented, but the damage done to child protection agencies following Cleveland and Waterhouse was immeasurable and irreversible. The media carefully picked up every point of criticism made by Lord Laming and devoted more story space to describing the role played by each agency than to the

1   The establishment of a government ministerial Children and Families
    Board.

2   The establishment of a National Agency for Children and Families,
    the Chief Executive of which will report to the ministerial Children
    and Families Board. The post of chief executive should incorporate
    the responsibilities of the post of a Children's Commissioner for
    England.

3   The National Agency for Children and Families to operate through
    a regional structure which will ensure that legislation and policy are
    being implemented at a local level.

4   The National Agency for Children and Families should, at their
    discretion, conduct serious case reviews (Part 8 reviews) or oversee
    the process.

5   The Management Board for Services to Children and Families must
    appoint a director responsible for ensuring that inter-agency
    arrangements are appropriate and effective.

6   Front-line staff in each of the agencies which regularly come into
    contact with families with children must ensure that, in each new
    contact, basic information about the child is recorded.

7   The Department of Health should amalgamate the current *Working
    Together* and the National Assessment Framework documents into
    one simplified document.

Figure 2.3 Laming Inquiry key recommendations
Source: Laming (2003)

perpetrators and their actions. Child protection agencies were truly on trial in the Climbie case, standing indirectly accused of the murder of an 8-year-old child through their indifference, incompetence and neglect. The media coverage suggested to the public that these professionals were somehow more culpable than the perpetrators: 'Murdered Victoria Failed 12 Times by her "Protectors"' (*Daily Mail*, 20 February, 2002).

Government response to the Laming Report and media focus

In the ensuing barrage of criticism the Labour Government had to respond quickly to the recommendations set out in the Laming Report. It did so in several key ways: first via the introduction of the

Green Paper Every Child Matters; second via the creation of a new government post, the Minister of State for Children,[2] and third via provisions in the Children Act 2004.

Every Child Matters: Change for Children is an initiative that seeks to address the well being of children and young people up to age 19. The initiative is built on the premise that every child is entitled to support in order to:

- Be healthy
- Stay safe
- Enjoy and achieve
- Make a positive contribution
- Achieve economic well-being.

(Every Child Matters website, DfES, 2007)

Following Laming, emphasis is placed upon effective inter-agency working to protect children and young people from harm and help them achieve. Following the Children Acts of 1989 and 2004 the focus is also upon the rights of children and young people to comment upon issues that affect them as individuals and collectively. Every local authority is required to work with its partners, through children's trusts, to explore effective working practice with children and young people in its area, and must act upon this information. In March 2005, the first Children's Commissioner for England was appointed. The Commissioner must actively seek the views of children and young people (with particular emphasis upon vulnerable children) and must promote their involvement in the work of organisations whose decisions and actions affect them. The government have also introduced the Common Assessment Framework (2005), a shared assessment tool in use across all children's services in England which aims to aid early identification of risk and need and to encourage effective inter-agency working. This is an attempt to standardise the previously *ad hoc* recording practice that existed within agencies. The government also plan to introduce a new child

2   The responsibilities of the post include: Sure Start, Early Years, Childcare, Connexions, LEA Special Education Needs and the Youth Service. The Children and Young People's Unit, Children's Social Services and the Teenage Pregnancy Unit, which will transfer from Department of Health. Responsibilities for family and parenting law and support (transferred from the Lord Chancellor's Department). The Family Policy Unit (10 Downing Street.gov.uk, 2006).

database (Children's Information Sharing Index) from the end of 2008 to record and enable the sharing of basic information about children between agencies. The National Framework under the Every Child Matters: Change for Children programme identifies ten key points in work with vulnerable children (Figure 2.4).

Laming appeared to be impressed with the range of measures introduced and proposed by the government in his presentation to child protection practitioners at an Every Child Matters Conference in 2005:

> The Green Paper 'Every Child Matters' set about a substantial reform in the way in which we view the needs of children and young people and families and the way in which we ensure their proper development. It also recognised that the vast majority of children are best cared for and best brought up in a secure home provided by their own families. And therefore the government has introduced a series of initiatives aimed at supporting families and the new Children Act 2004 has embedded this whole approach in legislation.
>
> (Laming, 2005)

---

1 Agencies have a duty to cooperate to promote the well-being of children

2 Agencies have a duty to make arrangements to safeguard and promote the welfare of children and young people

3 The development of statutory local safeguarding children boards (LSCBs) to replace non-statutory area child protection committees (ACPCs)

4 The appointment of local directors of children's services

5 The National Service Framework for Children and Young People

6 The Outcomes Framework

7 The development of an integrated inspection framework

8 The appointment of a Children's Commissioner

9 The development of a Common Assessment Framework

10 Workforce reform to help develop skills and ensure staffing levels

---

Figure 2.4 Every Child Matters
Source: www.everychildmatters.gov.uk/content/documents

However, Laming went on to express concern that the lack of inter-agency cooperation and communication he had pointed to had not been effectively addressed. Making direct reference to the Waterhouse Report, Laming suggested that effective communication between agencies regarding vulnerable children was of paramount importance in ensuring that more children did not become 'lost' in the care system.

This concern may not be misplaced, as a recent survey of NHS acute Hospital Trusts, conducted by Catherine Jacob, a Five News correspondent, suggests that many of the trusts had not implemented the recommendations of the Laming Report. The *Daily Mail* seized upon this survey with the headline 'Key Climbie Recommendations not Implemented' (22 May 2006). The *Mail* goes on to cite interviews undertaken by Jacob with the parents of Victoria Climbie and concerns expressed by Victoria's father regarding lack of communication between the agencies (*Daily Mail*, 22 May 2006).

The *Guardian* newspaper covered the government's planned introduction of the Child Index, explaining that all children (approximately 11 million) in England will be registered on an electronic database by the end of 2008, which will be accessible to all professionals involved in work with children (*Guardian*, 8 December 2005).[3] The story was given a positive spin, but writing for the *Guardian* Liz Davies (2006) took a more critical line regarding the introduction of the database (Children's Information Sharing Index). In an article dated 13 September 2006 she claimed that such a database may be open to hacking by sex offenders and to others who might sell on the information to abusers. Davies claims that the Children's Information Sharing Index (which will be operational in all areas by the end of 2008) will not protect vulnerable children from harm. Davies also claims that the Every Child Matters agenda is government rhetoric that will in reality fail to protect vulnerable children.

The Every Child Matters website (maintained by the DfES) does, however, state that every attempt will be made to seek children's

---

3   The index was created under s 12 of the Children Act 2004. The index will store basic information on children aged under 18 (under 21 where a young person has a mental health concern) including: gender, age, address and contact with agencies. The database will also contain information about children's parents/ carers (Hansard, 28 November, 2006).

views in operating the database, via an 'age-appropriate range of engagement strategies' (Every Child Matters, DfES, 2006, p 10). This 'engagement' does not extend to seeking views regarding the design of the database or the nature of the information held, as it already exists, but rather would seem to be a public relations exercise to gain the understanding and support of children and their parents, who in reality appear to have little say in the matter.

In true Every Child Matters style the government commissioned a small-scale study to explore what children and young people thought about the proposed index, and were probably disappointed to learn that young people did not want personal information stored on such a database: many expressed concern about the possibility of sex offenders and other agencies gaining access to personal information. The research was conducted by Hilton and Mills (2006) of the NSPCC, on behalf of the Office of the Children's Commissioner. Focus groups were conducted with 71 young people in England and Wales, all of whom had previously had some contact with child protection welfare services. Findings suggest that: young people were concerned about the nature and accuracy of the information to be stored on the new Children's Information Sharing Index; expressed doubts regarding the confidentiality and security of the database; were concerned about the possibility of being labelled and that information sharing may exacerbate their family or school situation; felt strongly that they should be consulted about the information stored about them, unless the risk was perceived to be extremely high; expressed concern about the sharing of information with schools where this may be used in bullying situations. Some of the respondents suggested that this may deter them from disclosing abuse to practitioners and discussing their problems. The report recommends that the DfES, and other government departments responsible for the control and maintenance of the index, give serious consideration to the key findings. The government's response has been to limit access to the index to professionals working in the child protection system and other relevant agencies, missing the point made by Davies (2006) and the young people responding to the survey – that sex offenders would probably be able to hack into the system, thus gaining access to sensitive personal information, or would be prepared to pay for information from the index. Hilton and Mills (2006) suggest on the basis of their research that:

practitioners and policy makers still have much to do to win the confidence of children and young people in the proposed computer system. The young people we spoke to also had strong views about information sharing in general and policy makers and practitioners need to listen to their voices to ensure that arrangements for information sharing work effectively and in the interests of children and young people.

(2006, p 1)

Indeed the government would do well to *really* listen to and take account of the views of children and young people in developing initiatives that directly affect their lives.

Children's access to justice: why aren't child sexual abuse cases prosecuted?

It is possible that child protection professionals, demoralised by the outcome of successive child abuse inquiries and hostile media attention, have become increasingly cautious in the identification and prosecution of alleged cases of child sexual abuse, as few cases are convicted. This might suggest reluctance on the part of the CPS to prosecute such cases in the absence of a guilty plea or conclusive evidence. Indeed, research has suggested that a significant number of cases involving child sexual abuse are categorised as 'no crime' and never considered by the CPS; 68 per cent of cases were categorised in this way in recent research conducted by Davidson et al. (2006). It is increasingly clear that a large number of sexual abuse cases reported to the police do not result in a conviction. The small number of convictions in child abuse cases may be accounted for by factors such as the difficulty of obtaining evidence and the reliability of children's accounts as influenced by the child's developmental stage. It is obvious that obtaining children's evidence in a form acceptable to a court is extremely difficult, and that disclosure itself is often problematic for victims, although possibly somewhat easier with increasing age. Recent research conducted in Norway suggests that rates of disclosure of sexual abuse increase with victim age with only 50 per cent of 3–6-year-olds compared to 74 per cent of 11–14-year-olds disclosing abuse when questioned. The study also concludes that rates of disclosure were lower in intra-familial than non-familial abuse cases (Jensen et al., 2005). Thus reporting of abuse with family perpetrators and at preadolescent ages requires particular attention. Davis et al. (1999), in their research on the CPS, address the high rate of discontinuance of child sexual abuse cases and suggest that it is in part due to the failure of children to provide a clear account of the abuse that will be acceptable to a court. Mudaly and Goddard (2006) have argued that the adult view that children are unable to provide reliable accounts of their experience due to emotional immaturity often underpins investigative work and that, in their experience, children are often able to articulate their experiences confidently. It is argued that young victims often demonstrate significant strategic decision-making skills in disclosing and describing the abuse they have experienced and case study evidence from young victims is provided to support this claim.

Davis et al. (1999) concluded that the decision to prosecute was based upon the existence of a clear victim account of the alleged abuse. This is particularly problematic where children are unable to provide such an account. The researchers go on to say that many such allegations were made by children from 'troubled backgrounds' (1999, p 3), or who had experienced abuse on previous occasions. The research also criticised the lack of specialist training offered to child protection police officers and social workers who conduct investigative interviews with children.

Pilot research undertaken by Davidson, Bifulco, Thomas and Ramsey (2006) aimed to inform the development of professional practice and training in the sensitive area of interviewing child and young victims. The work was based on the analysis of documentary evidence from 53 consecutive case files from two London boroughs (December 2004–March 2006) around the circumstances of reported sexual abuse, and interviews with a small sample of police officers about practice in two London child protection teams. The research is worth reporting in some depth as it sheds light on failings in the early investigative process that directly contribute to the low rate of criminal conviction in child sexual abuse cases.

This preliminary research highlighted several key issues: first, there is substantially less literature on the child's experience of the investigative police process than on the validity of the process in achieving best evidence, although these two issues are inextricably linked. There is, however, substantial research material on methods of questioning children and children's responses in the interview situation. Second, analysis of police reports describing investigations of sexual abuse from age eight upwards demonstrated that most victims were female and aged 13–15. Although the largest proportion of alleged perpetrators were fathers or surrogate fathers, this rate was nearly matched by the proportion of perpetrators who were male peers, including siblings and cousins. The most common reporting source was social services, followed by reporting by the victim or the mother. Therefore in investigating such cases particular awareness of teenage girls' vulnerabilities are required, together with awareness of situations involving alleged perpetrators who are not only fathers/surrogate fathers and family friends but also a large proportion who are peers.

Third, the largest proportion of cases (68 per cent) were recorded as 'undetected crimes'. This was attributed by police child protection officers to a variety of factors, including the unwillingness of victims to participate in the process; the lack of physical evidence given the retrospective nature of many cases; the absence of the suspect and delays by the CPS in providing advice on charging. However, it was notable that detection related to reporting source – while a large proportion of cases were reported by social services, very few of these were classified as 'detected crimes', compared with over half of those reported by victim or the mother. While most victims were given Achieving Best Evidence (ABE) interviews, this constituted *all* of those whose cases were classified as detected crimes, but only 70 per cent of those recorded as undetected crimes. Thus the interview was a critical if not sufficient factor in crime detection. Two child protection police officers made the following comments:

> A lot of children don't want to make statements against their parents, their carers. (R 1)

> A lot of times it's kids saying, 'I'm not going to say anything against my mum or dad. I don't want them arrested or to go to jail.' If they start saying that, you can't go against their wishes. That starts the difficulties. Sometimes they'll be ABE'ed and then after that they'll say they don't want to go to court. (R 10)

> (Davidson et al., 2006, p 18)

Fourth, all child protection police officers receive ABE training, which is generally well regarded, but the training was reported as too short with insufficient training opportunities in child-interviewing techniques and lack of 'refresher' training. Some officers felt that gaining interview experience was much more valuable than formal training, but identified the need for mentoring/guidance from the outset of their posting. Two police officers made the following comments on ABE training:

> It structures my interviews, really. That I can go in and plan in my head more or less what the framework of the interview is going to be. I've done my own work in trying to keep myself abreast of current practices ... I would argue that my training's not up to date ... I would love some input on particular skills relating to interviewing children ... I would like a lot clearer and more focused training to deal with that issue of being able to draw things out of a child but without leading. (R 4)

> I think the training that we've had is adequate. Perhaps they should introduce refresher training for us, because there are times when you don't do these things for a long period of time. If we don't have refresher training, then perhaps we should be assessed on it, but I've never had an assessment stage. (R 9)

> (Davidson et al., 2006, p 14)

Fifth, multi-agency working in child abuse was seen as problematic, although this varied between the two police teams with one having a better relationship with social services than the other. Negative perceptions of social workers included high rates of social worker staff turnover, inexperienced staff and poor communication. However, it was also recognized that the police service itself in child protection had insufficient resourcing, lack of managerial support and recognition, high work-load and high staff turnover. The number of unresolved cases was seen as demoralizing, particularly given the amount of work expended on individual cases and the high rate of undetected cases. However, satisfaction with the work included the acknowledged hard work among the officers, good level of skills, and competence and satisfaction around positive results. The area of child sexual abuse was viewed as important by the officers involved, despite a perception that it was not valued by the police force in general and that the work was difficult. One officer commented:

> The authors made the following recommendations on the basis of these findings:
>
> 1   Synthesising best investigative interview practice with best child-centred interview practice in police training to improve the quality of evidence and crime detection;
>
> 2   Increasing appropriate training availability within the police and other services;
>
> 3   Improving interagency working and collaboration through increasing relevant and joint training and communication at all levels;
>
> 4   Exploring further the working of the CPS to improve performance and communication;
>
> 5   Actively and routinely seeking the views of children and young people to inform the development of training and practice.

Figure 2.4 Recommendations to the Crown Prosecution Service
Source: Davidson et al. 2006

As for me enjoying this work, no, there's nothing enjoyable about this, it's not good news this. Quite a lot of it is pretty mundane rubbish, where we seem to be mopping up social problems. On the other hand, we have these incredibly tragic, serious cases going on, and we have to do it, someone has to do it. So no, it's not an enjoyable experience at all. (R 8)

(Davidson et al., 2006, p 20)

There was also general criticism of the CPS. Officers commented upon its slow response, delays in making decisions and lack of communication. Some also expressed little confidence in some junior CPS lawyers. Officers also felt deskilled by recent legal changes which have removed the power of charging from the police. Two police officers made the following comments regarding the CPS:

I don't think they (the CPS) like making decisions about child abuse. (R 5)

They've lost their way. The CPS – they're all overworked to start with. Personally, I think there will always be a role for the CPS. What is happening generally is, we're not investigating matters anymore. Prior to charge we are, as soon as the charge bit is finished, the CPS take over the job. Through lack of experience, they're making demands of us that are unreasonable and unnecessary. . . . They're recruiting kids up there who have just come out of law school, and they don't have a clue. And the ones who do have a clue are overworked. They seem too stressed out to take stuff on board. The system's wrong, not the personnel. The wrong sort of resourcing. They need to get it right. It's a big bugbear. (R 8)

(Davidson et al., 2006, pp 17–18)

What support is available for child victims?

There has already been extensive documentation of the experience of child witnesses in court proceedings by the Scottish Executive (1995). This has advocated an integrated witness support structure to augment the services available to young witnesses. As well as recommending extensive information and explanation for families and the judiciary, it also includes codes of practice for the legal profession and the creation of independent Child Witness Officer support figures as a central point for information and advice, and to prepare children for the court. The recommendations also sought to influence interviews and precognitions by restricting the number of times child witnesses were asked to discuss the circumstances of the alleged offence and to be aware of the stress caused by multiple interviews.

Plotnikoff and Woolfson (2001) undertook an evaluation of a child witness support role of an intermediary to assist communication with vulnerable witnesses at the investigative interview, or at trial, in six pathfinder areas. The research found that the intermediary scheme had not been well integrated into the work of local criminal justice organisations, with action plans and local monitoring frameworks still in development. This was in large part due to 'witness initiative overload'. However, when intermediaries were in place the matching of skills to witness needs worked well, with both intermediaries and police officers stating that the intermediaries' contribution at investigative interview was most valuable when planned in advance. The many advantages of the scheme included: higher rates of conviction; greater access to justice, with double the number of cases reaching trial; avoidance of miscarriages of justice; and facilitating communications at trial with help for witnesses to respond effectively. There were a number of benefits cited at the investigative stage, including the identification of poor comprehension by witnesses, saving time by informing decisions where it was not possible to proceed to interview and assisting at the efficient planning of interviews. Assisting witnesses at identification procedures, helping inform CPS decisions about witness suggestibility and ability to cope with cross-examinations, and how the witness should give evidence were also cited as positive outcomes. Despite these clear benefits, pathfinder areas had difficulties in identifying eligible witnesses, and there were low levels of requests for the intermediary appointments. This evaluation provides a valuable insight into the intermediary scheme and the impact of this upon the investigative process, highlighting problematic areas; however, the authors concluded that there were problems in rolling out the scheme. Indeed the scheme is at present very limited and has yet to be introduced to the London area.

In reality there is little support available for child victims of sexual abuse and their families. Police investigation of child sex abuse cases has to steer a difficult course between optimising the investigation of abusive events in order to 'achieve best evidence' and to satisfy the CPS, and attending to the child's developmental level, emotional and psychological state. In terms of the process this may mean reviewing the nature of inter-agency communication and joint training initiatives to enable efficient sharing of key information and to impart understanding about the distinctive nature of roles and boundaries across organisations.

Key chapter themes

- Successive child abuse inquiries have highlighted the shortcomings of the child welfare system, most notably Butler-Sloss (Cleveland); Waterhouse (Welsh children's homes) and Laming (Victoria Climbie).

- Media reporting and coverage of such inquiries has laid blame with social welfare agencies, criminal justice agencies and the government.

- The government have developed a range of new measures via the Children Act 2004 and the Every Child Matters framework in response to this criticism. The extent to which these measurse will address fundamental problems with practitioner training, retention and resourcing is questionable.

- Few allegations of child sexual abuse result in a criminal conviction. Factors such as: the reliability of children's testimony; the willingness of children to participate in criminal proceedings; lack of evidence; and poor inter-agency communication may be responsible for this.

References

Batty, D, 'Inexperienced social worker left to make complex decisions', *Guardian*, 28 September 2001

Batty, D, 'Chaotic department lost track of Victoria', *Guardian*, 5 October 2001

Batty, D, 'Climbie PC shirked visit for fear of scabies', *Guardian*, 19 November 2001

Brindle, D, 'Hunt for care workers in child abuse scandal', *Guardian*, 11 October 2000

Butler, P, 'Overstretched childcare service unraveled', *Guardian*, 18 October 2001

Butler-Sloss, E, 'Report of the Inquiry into Child Abuse in Cleveland in 1997', 1988, London: HMSO

'Climbie child protection "disgrace"', *Daily Mail*, 7 November 2001

Climbie, J, 'Key Climbie proposals "still not implemented"', *Daily Mail*, 22 May 2006

Cohen, S, *Folk Devils and Moral Panics: Creation of Mods and Rockers*, 3rd edn, 2002, London: Routledge

Davidson, J, Bifulco, A, Thomas, G and Ramsey, M, 'Placing the child at the centre of police practice and procedure: First stage final report to the Metropolitan Police Child Abuse Investigation Command', 2007, University of Westminster; Royal Holloway, University of London: London

Davidson, J, Bifulco, A, Thomas, G and Ramsey, M, 'Child victims of sexual abuse: Children's experience of the investigative process in the criminal justice system', *Practice Journal*, 18 (2006), pp 267–74

Davies, L, 'Data also needs protection', *Guardian*, 13 September 2006

Davis, G, Hoyano, L, Keenan, C, Maitland, L and Morgan, R, 'The admissability and sufficiency of evidence in child abuse prosecutions', 1999, Research Findings No 100: Home Office

Department for Education and Skills, 'Every child matters: Delivering change for children', 2004, accessed November 2007, www.everychildmatters.gov.uk/_content/documents

Department for Education and Skills, 'Common assessment framework', 2006, www.everychildmatters.gov.uk/deliveringservices/caf/

Doughty, S, 'Murdered Victoria failed 12 times by her "protectors"', *Daily Mail*, 20 February, 2002

Every Child Matters website, 2006, accessed March 2007, www.everychildmatters.gov.uk/socialcare/

Hall, S, Critcher, C, Jefferson, T, Clark, J and Roberts, B, *Policing the Crisis: Mugging, the State and Law and Order*, 1978, Macmillan: London

Hansard, accessed January 2007, www.publications.parliament.uk/pa/cm200607/cmhansrd/cm061128/text/61128w0003.htm

Hilton, Z and Mills, C, 'I think it's about trust: The views of young people on information sharing', 2006, Office of the Children's Commissioner, www.childrenscommissioner.org/documents/Report_VulnerableChildren_InfoSharing_NSPCCIndexRep_0%201.pdf

Jensen, T, Gulbrandsen, W, Mossige, S, Reichelt, S and Tjersland, O, 'Reporting possible sexual abuse: A qualitative study on children's perspectives and the context for disclosure', *Child Abuse and Neglect*, 29 (2005), pp 1395–413

Kelly, L, *Surviving Sexual Violence*, 1988, Oxford: Blackwell

'Key Climbie recommendations not implemented', *Daily Mail*, 22 May 2006

Laming, Lord, opening address at Every Child Matters Conference, 3 March 2005

'Legal action set to go all the way to Scotland's highest court', *Scotsman*, 11 September 2006

Mudaly, N and Goddard, C, *The Truth is Longer than a Lie: Children's Experiences of Abuse and Professional Interventions*, 2006, Jessica Kingsley: London

National service framework for children, young people and maternity services, 2004, accessed January 2007, www.dh.gov.uk/PolicyAndGuidance/HealthAndSocialCareTopics/ChildrenServices/ChildrenServicesInformation/fs/en

Neate, P, *Child Abuse: Scare in the Community, Britain in a Moral Panic*, 1995, Reed Business Publishing: London

Palmer, A, 'The people who failed Victoria', *Daily Telegraph*, 9 October 2001

Plotnikoff, J and Woolfson, R, 'An evaluation of child witness support', 2001, The Scottish Executive Central Research Unit, London: NSPCC

Saraga, E, 'Children's needs: Who decides?', in Langan, M (ed), *Welfare Needs, Rights and Risks*, 1998, London: Routledge

Scottish Executive, 'An evaluation of child victim support – Annex B the Lord Advocate's working group report and recommendations', 1995, accessed March 2007, www.scotland.gov.uk/cru/kd01/purple/witness-1.3.htm

The Times online, accessed 10 January 2007, www.timesonline.co.uk

Victoria Climbie Inquiry, 'Report of an Inquiry by Lord Laming', 2003, accessed December 2006, www.victoria-climbie-inquiry.org.uk/finreport/finreport.htm

Wallace, M, 'Disgrace of the bosses who let Victoria die', *Sun*, 29 January 2003

Waterhouse, R (2000), 'Lost in care: Report of the Tribunal of Inquiry into the abuse of children in care in the former county council areas of Gwynedd and Clwyd since 1974', accessed 10 November 2007, www.dh.gov.uk/en/Publicationsandstatistics/Publications/Publications PolicyAndGuidance/Browsable/DH_4928354

Wooding, D, 'Victoria file was altered', *Sun*, 23 November 2001

'Youngsters in care still at risk, says abuse report', *The Times*, 11 October 2000

Chapter 3

Understanding child sexual abusers and the impact of key cases

This chapter seeks to:

- Explore what is known about male and female child sexual abusers and their motivations for offending.

- Explore what is known about internet sex offenders.

- Consider media representations of two key cases involving the murder of children by known sex offenders and the subsequent impact upon populist notions and sexual abuse and upon government policy with sex offenders.

What do we know about child sexual abusers?

Child sexual abuse is a hidden crime, and if it is difficult to establish the true prevalence of such offending, it is even more difficult to comment with certainty on offender characteristics. Research has inevitably focused upon those perpetrators within the criminal justice system; either in custody or subject to community supervision.

No association between child sexual abuse and key variables such as social class and ethnicity is demonstrated in the research literature (Baker and Duncan, 1985). On a contradictory note, some research does indicate that abuse tends to be associated with social deprivation (La Fontaine, 1988). But this is largely attributed within the literature to the nature of investigations – Gorry's (1986)

British research looked at the manner in which offences involving incest become known to the police. He found that the majority of such offences were discovered accidentally when the police were investigating other crimes. The limited available research shows no association between child sexual abuse and level of intelligence, educational background, age and psychiatric status (Wolf, 1984).

Research conducted by the author with a sample of 119 convicted child sexual abusers subject to probation supervision suggested that perpetrators were aged between 31 and 40, with a mean average age of 36. This agrees with much of the research literature on convicted populations. Nash and West (1985) calculated a mean age of 34, and Finkelhor (1984) gives a figure of 27.9. The majority of offenders were male (96 per cent). Approximately half the group were employed in non-manual or skilled occupations (49 per cent); the remainder were either unemployed (25 per cent) or engaged in unskilled employment (26 per cent). This would seem to support the contention that there is no strong link between child sexual abuse and social class (La Fontaine, 1988). In 21 per cent of cases the offender's employment clearly involved close proximity to children. This may suggest that some were actively targeting children via their work. The majority (66 per cent) were or had been married or cohabiting at some point, while 42 per cent were married or cohabiting in a heterosexual relationship and with children at the time of the offence. Although the majority had children of their own (65 per cent), a minority of offenders claimed never to have been involved in an adult sexual relationship (34 per cent). A clear majority had no previous convictions for sexual offences (69 per cent) or other offences (68 per cent). Some 18 per cent of offenders claimed to have been actively involved in an abuser ring.

In 44 per cent of cases alcohol was identified as a contributory factor: perpetrators claimed that they drank a substantial amount prior to offending. While there is certainly some evidence to support this contention both from the existing literature (Aarens et al., 1977) and from the qualitative findings, it could be, following Gudjonsson (1987), that offenders were seeking to attribute blame internally at this stage in the court process. In the majority of cases (76 per cent) the offence occurred either in the perpetrator's home or in the victim's home (or both where incest was committed). The qualitative research demonstrated that many offenders are unwilling to take responsibility for their actions, even where a guilty plea is entered. Probation officers asked respondents who or what they felt was to blame for their behaviour. Of those pleading guilty, 71 per cent did not accept any responsibility and blamed their partner, the victim or both for their behaviour (Davidson, 2001).

Female sex offenders

Research literature indicates that child sexual abuse is an offence that women are much less likely to perpetrate than men (Salter, 1988; Fisher, 1994). Fisher (1994) states that during 1993 there were approximately 3,000 male sex offenders in British prisons, compared to only 12 female sex offenders. Home Office figures suggest that in 2005 the number of female sex offenders in England and Wales increased to 59, compared to 4,747 males (Home Office, 2007). Little is known about the nature of female sexual offending, and where research has been conducted it has tended to be of a case study nature given the small sample sizes (Barnett et al., 1990; Matthews, 1989; Elliot, 1993).

It is therefore assumed that women do not commit sexual offences against children. Research demonstrates that women are more likely to be convicted of offences involving the physical abuse of children than are men (Madden and Wrench, 1977). If it is the case that more women sexually abuse children than is believed, why are they not caught? In self-report studies where the victims are male, such as that conducted by Kelly et al. (1991) of British students, a fairly high rate of abuse on the part of females is reported. Also of interest is Kelly's finding that 62 per cent of those males reporting abuse on the part of a female stated that they were not traumatised by the offence/s. Finkelhor and Russell (1984) have suggested that such abuse may be less traumatic as females may use less force. It is probably more likely, however, that the prevailing culture of masculinity makes men less willing to admit to being abused. Although Coulborn-Faller's research (1993) suggests that more adult men are coming forward regarding their experiences of sexual abuse on the part of a female carer. Fromouth (1983) has suggested that males may be less likely to recognise the act/s as being abusive when victimised by females. This is attributed to cultural norms regarding masculinity and heterosexual relations.

Estimates of the incidence of female child sexual abuse have varied from 5–16 per cent of abuse perpetrated (Finkelhor and Russell, 1984; Faller, 1990). Finkelhor and Russell (1984) used secondary analysis of existing data from the American Humane Society and the National Incidence Study in order to study the incidence of female child sexual abuse. Unfortunately the definition of sexual abuse adopted by the two sources was so different as to make comparison difficult. The focus was upon only those females who had committed sexually abusive acts against children, while excluding those who had 'allowed' the offences to occur (presumably when perpetrated by males). Finkelhor and Russell found that six per cent of female victims had been abused by a female perpetrator compared to 14 per cent of male victims. The little research that has been conducted regarding the nature of sexual offending against children by women has tended to suggest that they offend with males: Barnett et al. (1990) found that all six of the women in their treatment group had offended with male accomplices.

Abusers tend to be male, and empirical evidence suggests that this is so – why should this be the case? Some have suggested that the key to understanding this lies in the physiology of the act: a woman cannot have sexual intercourse with a man unless his penis is erect. This is not within a woman's control (Walters, 1975). This, however, shows a certain lack of understanding of child sexual abuse, given that some abuse involves masturbation and not full sexual intercourse, which could be equally gratifying to a woman. Finkelhor (1979, 1984) has suggested that women have a different type of relationship with children than do men. They have more physical contact with children, which is described as 'freer' (p 77) as it is permitted.

Coulborn-Faller's (1993) review of the literature on convicted female child sexual abusers provides a useful insight into the characteristics of such women. She describes the majority of female perpetrators as 'very dysfunctional' and states that their offences are frequently associated with a high incidence of mental disorder, substance misuse and parenting difficulties. Often, it would seem, where sexual abuse is perpetrated by women, it is accompanied by neglect and physical and emotional abuse. The literature reviewed suggests that a large proportion of offences perpetrated by women were done so with others in the context of the extended family. Here children were sometimes used for pornography or prostitution; when 'lone abuse' was perpetrated it tended to be within a marriage or stable relationship. Several studies also reported cases of 'lone abuse' where a woman was living without a constant male partner and the eldest male child, having taken over the male adult role, was subjected to sexual abuse on the part of their mother. Coulborn-Faller also created a category to describe adolescent female offenders, who tended to be 'inadequate' and have difficulty in building and maintaining peer relationships, selecting children as a substitute for peers. The other circumstances under which females abuse are described as 'ritual': here, ritual abuse was practiced in groups, many of which were religious, including both women and men. The final group consisted of professional carers who were accused of sexual abuse by the children in their care. A study conducted by Elliot (1993) explored the accounts of 127 adult respondents who were sexually abused by a woman as children. The respondents reported similarly negative effects to those of victims abused by men. The majority (78 per cent) who did report the sexual abuse at the time were not believed and could find little help. More recent research undertaken by Warren and Hislop (2006), which has identified a spate of cases involving female perpetrators and adolescent boys, suggests that women are abusing for their own gratification and not acting only as facilitators for men. Warren and Hislop (2006, pp 425–8), in their research with female sexual offenders, have developed a typology of female sexual abusers:

1   'Facilitators' – women who intentionally aid men in gaining access to children for sexual purposes.
2   'Reluctant partners' – women in long-term relationships who go along with sexual exploitation of a minor out of fear of being abandoned.
3   'Initiating partner' – women who want to sexually offend against a child and who may do it themselves or get a man or another woman to do it while they watch.
4   'Seducers and lovers' – women who direct their sexual interest towards adolescents and develop an intense attachment.
5   'Paedophiles' – women who desire an exclusive sexual relationship with a child.
6   'Psychotic' – women who suffer from a mental illness and who have inappropriate sexual contact with children as a result.

Warren and Hislop comment that many of the women in their research came from chaotic backgrounds. The existing research presents an image of female sex offenders as assisting male offenders, and has linked female sexual abuse to poor mental health. There have been several recent cases in the UK involving women in positions of trust,[1] and similar cases in the United States, which suggest that some

1	A 35-year-old woman, married with two children, arrested for having sexual relations with a 16-year-old male.
2	A teacher received a prison sentence for raping a male student.
3	A teacher accused of indecent assault on a 14-year-old male student.
4	A teacher accused of indecent assault on a 12-year-old boy.
5	A teacher pleaded guilty to sexual assault charges on three male students.
6	A teacher pleaded guilty to rape and performing a criminal sexual act on a 16-year-old student. Sentenced to six months in custody and placed on the sex offenders register.
7	A teacher received a two-year probation sentence for sending obscene images and texts to a 16-year-old student.

Figure 3.1 US case studies of female abusers
Source: Adapted from LaRue, Concerned Women For America (2006)

educated middle-class women have been forming abusive relationships with their students, on their own volition. The Legal Studies section of the *Concerned Women for America* website lists several such cases in the United States (Figure 3.1), which all involve female teachers and male students.

While it would seem that men are more likely to sexually abuse children than women, the true extent of female sexual abuse is unknown and further research is needed. Recent cases involving female perpetrators seem to indicate that women are more likely to abuse teenagers, rather than younger children, but more research is needed. It is clear, however, that a significant number of women do commit such offences, and to characterise child sexual abuse as an exclusively male crime is to marginalise the few female offenders that do enter the criminal justice system and ensure that little substantial treatment provision is available to them. There are currently no treatment programmes available for female sex offenders in UK prisons.

1   Note for example the case of Debbie Lane, 35, in Scotland, a childminder who sent explicit mobile phone texts to a boy of 13, and who escaped a prison sentence (March 2007) after a sheriff said there were no sex-offender programmes for women in prison. She was instead ordered to serve 200 hours community service.

Male sex offenders

A growing awareness regarding the high incidence of child sexual abuse and the harmful consequences to the victim during the 1980s and 1990s has resulted in a proliferation of research on male abusers. However, little is really known about what distinguishes male abusers from non-abusers; what motivates them to offend and how frequently they offend. Research has relied upon male offenders self-reporting (Kaplan, 1985; Abel and Becker, 1987) – the reliability of such work has been questioned, given the extent of the denial and minimisation associated with child sexual abuse which throws doubt upon offender's own accounts.

Some have stressed the importance of confidentiality and immunity from prosecution in ensuring accurate findings (Kaplan, 1985), and some researchers have been able and willing to make such guarantees (Abel and Becker, 1987, for example). While it may be the case that better research will result from confidentiality (and this is usually a most important ethical consideration when undertaking research) the morality of concealing information regarding sexual offences committed against children can be questioned. Other variables are important in determining how forthcoming abusers are in interview. Abel et al. (1983) suggest that interviewer style and experience makes a difference – they found that subjects were much more willing to discuss their offending and offending history when re-interviewed by a more experienced interviewer.

Abel and Becker's (1987) self-report recidivism study of 561 non-incarcerated sex offenders remains the most comprehensive to date. Conducted in the United States the study provides an overview of the characteristics of male abusers. The respondents were aged from 13–76 years, with a mean age of 31.5 years. The majority were employed and had formed a stable relationship with an adult partner (married or cohabiting). In keeping with other research, the ethnic origin and social class of the sample was representative of the general population. The majority had committed offences against female children.

The offenders reported a large number of offences: some 291,737 sexual acts were said to have been perpetrated against 195,407 victims; 153 child sexual abusers (non-familial offences against male children) admitted to 43,100 offences involving 22,981 victims, constituting an average of 282 offences per offender and an average of 150 victims each (cited in Barker and Morgan, 1993). The majority of respondents (53.6 per cent) also reported the onset of deviant sexual interest before their eighteenth birthday. In support of Abel and Becker's research, Weinrott and Saylor (1991) interviewed institutionalised child sexual abusers (and other sex offenders) and found that many undetected sexual offences were disclosed.

Age appears to be an important variable: studies point to an age range from early adolescence upwards, with a mean average age of 30–35 (Nash and West, 1985). Increasingly, however, and in support of the then-controversial findings of Abel et al. (1988) that the onset of deviant behaviour can occur prior to age 18, research has increasingly focused upon adolescent abusers, and this reflects a boom during the 1990s in treatment programmes specifically aimed at such abusers (O'Callaghan and Print, 1994). Is such a focus justified? A prevalence survey conducted by Kelly et al. (1991) in England and Wales, in which a sample of 1,244 16–21 year olds were surveyed, concluded that 27 per cent of perpetrators were aged between 13 and 17 years. While similar research conducted by the Northern Ireland Research Team (1991) reviewed 408 cases of child sexual abuse and found that in 36.1 per cent of cases the abuser was an adolescent. Some research comparing adolescent sex offenders to other adolescent offenders has generally failed to find any significant differences between the two groups (Smith, 1988; Oliver, 1993). Fagan and Wexler (1988), for example, found that adolescent abusers were as likely to come from stable homes (defined as living with both natural parents) and had low reported rates of substance abuse. Becker and Kaplan (1988) found that adolescent abusers were less likely to have encountered the criminal justice system. Oliver's (1993) study comparing a group of adolescent abusers to a group of adolescent offenders committing property-related crimes found that the abusers were least likely to have a recognised mental health problem and showed fewer deviant characteristics (assessed by psychometric testing) than the non-abusing group. The only other difference between the two groups was that the abusers tended to score higher on measurements of inter-personal maturity. Other research has contradicted such findings in suggesting that such offenders tend to come from 'dysfunctional' families and may have experienced physical or sexual abuse (Kear-Colwell, 1996; Graves et al., 1996; Smallbone and Dadds, 1998; Ward and Keenan, 1999; Briggs and Kennington, 2006). There is an increasing amount of recent research into the characteristics of adolescent sex offenders – all such studies are based upon small samples of young offenders currently in the criminal justice system (Almond et al., 2006; Hutton and White, 2006; Moultrie, 2006).

Internet sex offenders

Sex offenders use the internet to access indecent images of children, to select victims for abuse and to communicate with other sex offenders. Police officers have suggested that there is a great and increasing demand for indecent images of children and that it is increasingly difficult to track down the child victims and the perpetrators involved (Davidson, 2007).

Internet sex offender behaviour can include: the construction of sites to be used for the exchange of information, experiences and indecent images of children; the organisation of criminal activities that seek to use children for prostitution purposes and that produce indecent images of children at a professional level; the organisation of criminal activities that promote sexual tourism (Davidson and Martellozzo, 2007). Indecent images of children are frequently shared by sex offenders using the internet, and the industry in such images is becoming increasingly large and lucrative (Wyre, 2003). Taylor, Holland and Quayle (2001) suggest that some online sex offenders are 'collectors' of indecent images of children, who routinely swap images with other collectors; it is also suggested that some of these images are photographs taken by people known to the children, such as members of their family (Quayle, cited in Davidson, 2007), although at present there is little empirical evidence to support this claim, and more research is needed.

Quayle and Taylor (2003) also comment on the possible motivations of online child sex abusers. It is suggested that sex offenders perceive the internet as a means of generating an immediate solution to their fantasies. Factors including presumed anonymity, disinhibition and ready accessibility undoubtedly encourage offenders to go online. Quayle and Taylor (2003) also acknowledge, however, that the unique structure of the internet may play a major role in facilitating online child abuse. One practitioner respondent working with internet sex offenders has suggested that offenders' internet use is not limited to abuse, and that the internet often plays a significant role in other areas of their lives (Davidson, 2007).

A typology of internet child sex offenders has been developed by Krone (2004) – this has been adapted for use by Wortley and Smallbone (2006) to guide the work of police officers in the United States. While some of the categories are questionable, the typology does include those offenders targeting and grooming children online, a group largely excluded from other typologies. Nine categories of offender are identified: the first category are 'Browsers' (Wortley and Smallbone, p 15), offenders who *accidentally* come across indecent images and save them – in reality such images are either purchased via credit card or are swapped by collectors. The second category are 'Private fantasisers' (p 15), those who create digital images for their own private use. The third are 'Trawlers' (p 15), those who search for indecent images through open browsers and may engage in some networking. The fourth are 'Non-secure collectors' (p 15), offenders who look for indecent images in open areas of the internet such as chat rooms – they will probably be networking. The fifth are 'Secure collectors' (p 16), offenders who belong to an online, hidden, paedophile network; these offenders are highly organised, likely to be collectors and employ sophisticated security to conceal their offending. The sixth are 'Groomers' (p 16), offenders targeting and grooming children via peer-to-peer technology, interactive internet games and chat rooms; these offenders may send indecent images to children as a part of the grooming process. The seventh are 'Physical abusers' (p 16), contact abusers who have an interest in indecent images as a part of their fantasy cycle; these offenders may photograph their abusive behaviour for their own use. The eighth are 'Producers' (p 17), offenders who record the sexual abuse of children for the purposes of distribution to networks and to satisfy their own fantasy. The final category includes 'Distributors' (p 17), offenders distributing indecent images either for financial gain or as part of their collecting behaviour.

In summary it would appear that: child sexual abusers tend to be male, although women do perpetrate sexual offences against children (research addressing this issue is limited); the mean age of those abusers studied is between 30 and 35, although research is increasingly addressing adolescent abuse and the use of the internet to perpetrate abuse; no association appears to exist between the sexual abuse of children and social class, ethnic origin or geographical region; victims tend to be female.

Theorising child sexual abuse: exploring motivations

Numerous explanations have been offered regarding why male abusers sexually assault children. Explanations tend to be: physiological, focusing on brain abnormalities for example (Langevin, 1990);

psychological, pointing to the importance of early childhood experience (Kline, 1987); sociological, stressing the central role of structural factors such as power relations (Kelly, 1988); eclectic, combining sociological and psychological thought (Finkelhor, 1984). It is important to consider the theoretical context of abuse as current policy, sentencing and treatment practice has largely evolved from cognitive behavioural work.

Physiological and biological theories

The literature pointing to physiological explanations of sexual offending in males has tended to concentrate on offences involving adults, and has not attempted to explain why, if sexual offending is due to physiological factors and therefore beyond the control of perpetrators, abusers choose to assault children? There is very little research evidence to support such theories, although the area is under researched. Physiological theories have tended to focus on the existence of brain abnormalities and testosterone levels in male sex offenders in an attempt to explain sexual abuse. Langevin (1990) claimed to show a link between temporal lobe impairment and deviant sexual behaviour in male sex offenders. However, as Langevin points out, there is no way of knowing, particularly given the small number of cases involved in his experiment, if the relationship between sexually deviant behaviour and brain impairment is a causal one. Studies focusing upon testosterone levels in male sex offenders (testosterone is the hormone associated with arousability in males) assume that unusually high levels of the hormone prompt sexual abuse (Lanyon, 1991; Rada et al., 1976). Berlin and Hopkins (1981) have reported higher testosterone levels in a large number of child sexual abusers. Hucker and Bain (1990), in their review of the literature around this area, conclude that the majority of such studies should be treated with caution, as the broad generalisations made are in fact based on very small clinical samples and findings are often incomplete. The most damning criticism of this theoretical approach comes from research conducted in England and Wales (Beckett et al., 1994). The Home Office sponsored study compared the efficacy of seven community based treatment programmes for sex offenders, the majority of whom (53 of 58) were child sexual abusers. The study highlighted the success of long-term community-based programmes in enabling offenders to control their offending. The physiological approach assumes that offenders are unable to control their behaviour in the absence of medical treatment to reduce hormone levels; if this were the case other forms of behavioural treatment would not appear to be effective. It could of course be the case that abusers become more adept at evading detection as a consequence of attending a programme.

Freudian theory and child abuse

Psychology has made probably the most significant contribution to the study of child sexual abuse. Psychological theory ranges from the more traditional Freudian psychoanalytic school to recent cognitive behavioural theories. Psychoanalytic theory originates in the work of Sigmund Freud, and has had a great impact upon both the treatment and theoretical explanation of child sexual abuse. It was Freud's belief that all personality disorders, such as sexual deviance, arose from unresolved sexual problems in childhood. In Freud's later work, unsatisfactory resolution of the 'Oedipus complex' in males (the 'Electra complex' in females) was seen as one of the primary causes of sexual deviation. The Oedipus complex refers to the belief that male children desire sexual relations with their mother, wish their father dead and fear castration from their father by way of retribution. The child comes to resolve this dilemma through identification with the father and a happy relationship is resumed (Freud, 1952).

Adult sexual problems arise following the unsuccessful resolution of this complex in childhood. Post-Freudians such as Weldon (1988) have blamed the unsuccessful resolution of the Oedipus complex on poor parenting on the part of the mother, while others such as Kline (1987) point to the inadequate development of the superego, implying that childhood desires are taken into adult life and inappropriately directed towards children (Lanyon, 1991). The complexity of this theory makes it difficult to investigate empirically – the existence of higher rates of abuse among single parent households may give some credence to this theory, but there is no evidence to suggest that this is the case. The basis of post-Freudian claims has been challenged: first, Freudian theory has been criticised on methodological grounds, as it was based on the work conducted by Freud with a small number of middle-class Viennese women who may not be representative; second, post-Freudians such as Kline (1987) have failed to explain the existence of female child sexual abusers, focusing exclusively on males; third, while women as mothers are implicated in ultimately giving rise to abuse via the poor parenting of male children (Weldon, 1988), no consideration is given to the fact that victims tend to be female (Salter, 1988).

These criticisms are important, but do little to damage the respect enjoyed by Freudian theory. Other commentators go as far as to state that psychoanalytic theory has done irreversible damage to the study of child sexual abuse. Herman and Hirschman (1977) believe, for example, that Freud did much to detract from the seriousness of the problem. Freud's early theories of neurosis highlighted the significance of early childhood sexual experiences (Garcia, 1987). On finding that a large number of his female patients reported having been sexually abused at a young age by adults, he first stated that child sexual abuse was the root cause of all neurosis in adulthood. Freud called such abuse 'infantile seduction' (cited in Clark, 1982, p 156); the seduction of children on the part of adults. Freud recognised the trauma caused by such abuse, and went on to say that: 'Foremost among those guilty of abuses like these, with their momentous consequences, are nursemaids, governesses and domestic servants' (Freud, cited in Clark, 1982, p 156).

In this important observation Freud both recognises the harmful consequences of abuse and identifies the abusers as predominantly female. Freud also refers to strangers and other children as key perpetrators (Freud, 1896, p 164). Commenting on his work Masson (1984) notes that in his writing during the late 1800s Freud seemed hesitant in blaming fathers and other male relatives, but does so on many occasions in his letters to William Fliess. It would seem that Freud was reluctant to publicly acknowledge that sexual abuse was being perpetrated by men within families.

Freud later reconsidered his theory, probably in the light of criticism from colleagues. Clark (1982) recounts the first reading of Freud's theory on 'infantile seduction' in a lecture to the Society of Psychiatry and Neurology in Vienna. The reception the paper received is said to have been summed up by a comment made by the chair, Krafft-Ebing: 'it sounds like a scientific fairytale' (Clark, 1982, p 158). In the face of such open criticism Freud concluded that the accounts he had heard were fabricated, the fantasies of middle-class women. This lead to the formulation of the Oedipus and Electra complexes, which postulated a strong impulse in the child for sexual relations with the parent of the opposite sex (Hitschmann, 1921). Rush (1974) has argued that Freud reframed his original theory as he personally was unwilling to face the implication that the behaviour of his own peers lay behind his patients' problems. It is also likely that Freud did not wish to risk the condemnation of Viennese society at such an early stage of his career. Freud attempted to explain his retraction of the infantile seduction theory in a letter to William Fliess:

> The continual disappointment in my efforts to bring a single analysis to a real conclusion; the running away of people who for a period of time had been most gripped [by analysis]; the absence of the complete successes on which I had counted; (. . .) Then the surprise that in all cases, the father, not excluding my own, had to be accused of being perverse.
>
> (cited in Masson, 1985, p 264)

Freud may have been one of the first to stumble upon the extent of sexual abuse experienced during childhood, however the dismissal of patients' accounts as fantasy had catastrophic effects in that the ideology underlying psychoanalysis, from which psychiatric practice originates, discounted victims' experiences of childhood sexual abuse and succeeded in blaming children for the abuse they suffered (Masson, 1984, 1985). Indeed, Finkelhor (1986, p 9) has stated that: 'this ideology of denial and blaming the victim has been the biggest obstacle to the serious study and promotion of the problem of children's sexual victimisation'.

The influence of Freudian thought is widespread in present day psychology. Groth (in Lanyon, 1991), for example, has suggested that abusers are motivated by unresolved life issues occurring in childhood, and are characterised as either fixated or regressed. The fixated abuser has a consistent primary sexual interest in children, and is unable to maintain long-term relationships with adults. The regressed abuser has formed relationships with adults but will regress into relationships with children under certain circumstances, such as when rejected by an adult.Later psychoanalytic theories have focused upon the family. Mrazek (1981) claims that the absence of a good marital bond and previous incestuous behaviour on the part of male family members make for a dysfunctional family, in which incest is likely to occur, while De Young (1982) suggests that incest arises when discontented males, who are too inhibited to seek sexual gratification outside the family, abuse their daughters. The incest is viewed as symptomatic of the dysfunction. It could however be argued that the presence of a child-abusing male in any family unit would cause that family to become dysfunctional.

Treatment approaches do not now tend to locate the origins of abuse with the mother, as more has been discovered about the way in which male abusers target and manipulate children (Elliot et al., 1995). Freudian theory has tended to blame women for acts perpetrated by men; some later commentators have claimed that this tendency remains, and that professionals indirectly blame the mothers of abused children for not providing adequate protection. Carter (1999) suggests that 'mother blaming' plays a central role in Canadian child welfare legislation and policy, and as a consequence of this the women in her study came to blame themselves for their child's abuse: 'women in this study were blamed (and blamed themselves) for their children's victimisation. It was documented how institutionalised sexism contributed to the ethic of blame experienced by the mothers interviewed' (p 199).

Behavioural theory and child abuse

Behavioural learning theories within psychology originate in the early work of Pavlov in the late nineteenth century and Skinner in the 1920s (cited in Sparks, 1982), who studied learned responses to external stimuli among animals. Learning theorists attribute child sexual abuse to the misdirected learning of behaviour. In keeping with Pavlov's original study of the manner in which dogs could be conditioned to respond to external stimuli, learning theorists state that the sexual abuse of children occurs when abusers associate childlike characteristics with sexual arousal. Abusers may become aroused by a small childlike body, for example (Laws and Marshall, 1990): the impact of the stimulus is such that the characteristics become the prompt for sexual arousal. Other learning theorists, such as Wolf (1984), suggest that a childhood history of sexual, emotional or physical abuse leads to the development of an inclination towards sexual deviancy. It is suggested that through such experience children learn inappropriate behaviour; the abusive experiences serve to act as 'potentiators' for the child to learn inappropriate behaviour. Wolf states that the more potentiators there are, the greater the risk that the child will become a sex offender. The presence of potentiators coupled with other stimuli, such as alcohol, drugs or pornography, lead to deviant sexual fantasy, which provides the backdrop to future offending. According to Wolf, events leading to feelings of powerlessness and worthlessness reinforce deviant sexual fantasies, which are often masturbatory. This acts as a rehearsal for future offending. Wolf's theory has been applied in practice in treatment programmes in the UK and the United States (Barker and Morgan, 1993) for sex offenders, and Wolf's cycle of abuse theory continues to be used extensively in work with offenders. However, the theory can be criticised on a number of counts: first, self-report studies of child sexual abusers report rates of abuse perpetrated against offenders to be anywhere between 10 per cent and 50 per cent. Assuming that 50 per cent of abusers have themselves experienced abuse, the remaining 50 per cent have not, and therefore presumably could not have learned the behaviour. Second (a related point), all those who have experienced abuse do not necessarily abuse as adults: the fact that the majority of victims are female and the majority of perpetrators are male bears testimony to this. The behavioural approach underpins approaches to sex offender treatment in the UK, and has informed the development of cognitive behavioural programmes.

The term 'cognitive behavioural' is used in this context to describe a broad approach incorporating central themes. The approach has been adapted for use in sex offender treatment by Finkelhor (1984), but incorporates themes from other literature (Wolf, 1984, for example). The approach focuses upon the extent to which offenders seek to attribute blame to their victims, others and offence circumstances, rather than accept their role in the commission of the offences. The theory has been developed further by Gudjonssen (1987, 1990, 1991). Approaches to treatment are discussed in Chapter Five. Cognitive behavioural treatment has sought to enable offenders to accept responsibility for their own behaviour, and to understand the impact that their behaviour has had upon their victim. This approach also rests upon the assumption that offenders will have low self-esteem and be socially isolated individuals incapable of maintaining successful adult relationships. In practice, programmes seek to teach social skills, to raise confidence and to cause offenders to reflect upon the negative and positive aspects of past relationships. The programmes also aim to encourage the development of adult social activities. It is assumed that offenders have distorted attitudes towards children, in that children are viewed as sexual objects. This distortion is fuelled by the offender's lack of victim empathy and a tendency to fantasise sexually regarding the commission of deviant behaviour – the fantasising is often seen as a trigger to offending. Here deviant sexual fantasies regarding children are turned into reality when offenders act upon their thoughts. These key concepts are discussed below in the context of research findings from interview-based qualitative research conducted by the author with a small group (18) of convicted child sexual abusers subject to probation supervision (Davidson, 2001).

Self-esteem and social isolation

Low self-esteem has been identified as characteristic of sex offenders in the literature: Pithers (1999) states that 61 per cent of child sexual abusers in his research (the sample size is not given) had low self-esteem. Marshall (1996) also suggests that low self-esteem was characteristic of his sample of sex offenders, while Wolf (1984) describes the way in which low self-esteem contributes to the 'cycle of offending' in sex offenders. He suggests that offenders seek to compensate for this through sexual contact with children. Many of these studies have relied upon psychometric testing to measure the concept: questionnaires used have included statements with which offenders must agree or disagree. The difficulty here arises in identifying how far sex offenders are social isolates, who lack self-esteem from an early age, and how far their arrest, subsequent conviction and labelling cause them to be isolated from the rest of society as social outcasts. The absence of good peer relationships is apparent from offender accounts of their childhoods:

> My school days were lonely. I didn't really have friends, apart from my cousin who lived over the road. (G 2.6)

> Q: How would you describe your childhood?
> A: Unhappy, I think I was a very quiet child, not many friends really.
> Q: Did you have any close friends?
> A: No, no close friends. I didn't mind being on my own. (G 1.5)

> Q: How would you describe your schooldays?
> A: Hated every bit of it. Don't know why, I just didn't want to be there. I found it difficult to talk in large groups.
> Q: Did you have friends?
> A: No, I was always playing on my own and when I went home I used to play in the garden on my own. (G 1.2)
>
> (Davidson, 2001)

The author's research suggests that respondents experienced more isolation in their childhood than later in adult life. There is a sense in which the majority appeared 'lonely': while some may have had a number of friends with whom they could socialise, few had 'close' friends, and only two had a friend in whom they could confide. The concept of 'loneliness' is taken to be qualitatively different to that of 'isolation'. Loneliness has been defined by Peplau and Perlman (1982) as the subjective view that ones existing relationships lack depth and meaning. A person may have many social contacts but no meaningful relationships. Attachment theorists such as Bowlby (1973) and Rook (1985) have suggested that people wish to have relationships with those who they perceive will offer comfort and security. Individuals are seen to function best when they know that they have reliable others who provide consistent support in difficult times. Seen in these terms there was a distinct absence of such significant others in the lives of the respondents in this research – for some this was characteristic of their childhood years also. Finkelhor (1986) attributes sexual offending, in part, to the claim that abusers are said to be more emotionally congruent with children: the evidence from this research would suggest that, as children, respondents were not emotionally congruent with their peers and frequently experienced difficult relations with adults. The extent of social isolation experienced during childhood appeared to be considerable. The findings indicate that offenders were often lonely, isolated children. Low self-esteem did appear to be an enduring problem for this group of offenders, which was doubtless exacerbated by arrest, subsequent conviction and public labelling as a 'sex offender'. The findings from the research of Beckett et al. (1994) would appear to support this contention: prior to entering a treatment programme, their sample of abusers were characterised as 'emotionally isolated individuals lacking self-confidence. They were under-assertive, poor at appreciating the perspective of others and ill-equipped to deal with emotional distress'.

In the author's research the majority of the respondents described feelings of inadequacy at school coupled with low feelings of self-worth and a general lack of confidence in their academic ability. Respondents' comments illustrate this point:

I wasn't too good at school, I learnt more when I left. I felt a bit thick you know. (R 2.6)

[Respondent] I never felt I was academic, I still feel I was stupid and thick.

Q: Why did you feel that way?

A: I remember phrases, words you know. I just felt stupid, maybe because my sister was way ahead. (R 1.1)

How far such experiences are characteristic of child sexual abuser populations is questionable. The respondents did, however, recount descriptions of school bullying and peer abuse, which were associated with feelings of low self-worth and hopelessness:

Q: Why were you truanting?
A: Well, the usual thing, bullying. There was a gang of around six, they would wait for me after school; they would pick on me if I was in the way. They would often beat me up; I used to have cuts and bruises.
Q: Did you tell your parents?
A: They knew, but they didn't pay much attention. Dad said I should just get on with it and stand up to them. (R 1.7)

This respondent was 68 at the time of the interview – he said that he would never forget the abuse he suffered at school. Another respondent attributed feelings of worthlessness in childhood to his experiences both at school and at home. He describes a home environment in which he was frequently both physically and emotionally abused by his mother. He was asked to describe what kind of child he was:

A: I don't know [long pause], unhappy, I suppose.
Q: What made you unhappy?
A: If anyone walked into a classroom I knew that they would blame me; I knew that they would blame me for something. If anyone spoke to me I would blush. I was shy; my mother said that if a smaller kid shit on me I would stand there and take it.
Q: Do you think that's true?
A: Yes, that's the kind of kid I was. (R 1.1)

This would seem to indicate that the respondent did have very low self-esteem as a child, which he appears to attribute to both his experiences at home and at school. It is interesting that he agrees with his mother's description of him.

There is very little research addressing the family histories of child sexual abusers, although many writers have pointed to the importance of childhood experience in the development of a sexual attraction to children. Some have described the negative influence of living with a dysfunctional family (Graves et al., 1996; Smallbone and Dadds, 1998). Others have described the negative effect of frequent, inconsistent and severe punishment on the part of parents as contributing to the development of emotionally immature individuals who may sexually abuse children (Rada, 1978). This research lends weight to such work, and the early life-histories of the respondents reveal a high level of both physical and emotional abuse. There seems to be little doubt that many of the respondents experienced difficult and at times painful childhoods. The question does however remain: why do others have similar experiences and yet not go on to sexually abuse children?

Recent research that has explored the family histories of sex offenders has pointed to the problems associated with attempting to make causal links. Graves et al. (1996), in their study of the parental characteristics of juvenile sex offenders, concluded that: 'thus the overall findings suggest that whereas the majority of sex offenders come from homes employing pathological interaction, there were some who came from homes coded as "healthy"' (p 310). If we were seeking to establish a causal link between a poor early home environment and sexual offending, it would be difficult to account for the minority of sex offenders in Graves's (1996) study who came from secure family backgrounds (where there was no evidence of emotional or physical abuse and no evidence of parental addiction to drugs or alcohol).

Other research has been equally cautious in suggesting a link: Smallbone and Dadds (1998), in their study of early attachment to parental figures, have stated tentatively that 'early insecure attachment experiences may place some men at risk of later (sexual) offending' (p 571). The author's research also suggests that such experiences within the nuclear family were compounded by experiences at school – these factors were seen as contributing to feelings of low self-esteem and self-worth. There is little direct research addressing the school experiences of sex offenders. Some writers have, however, suggested that child sexual abusers are likely to have experienced insecure childhood attachments, as a consequence of which they may build insecure adult relationships (Ward and Keenan, 1995). These insecure attachments have been attributed largely to poor relations with parents or primary carers: these relations have been characterised as being unresponsive, rejecting and physically abusing of children (Smallbone and Dadds, 1998). A large amount of research into the family backgrounds of juvenile sex offenders has been undertaken by psychologists. Findings indicate that: parents or carers tended to be distant or inaccessible (Smith and Israel, 1987); families displayed high levels of mental illness and instability (Bagley, 1992); a large proportion of parents had suffered considerable physical or sexual abuse as children – Lankester and Meyer's (1986) research, for example, suggested that 64 per cent of the parents of their sample of 153 juvenile sex offenders had such experiences. It is possible that these insecure attachments extended to school and relationships with peers also, although there is little research evidence to suggest that this is the case.

Adult relationships

The assumption underpinning cognitive behavioural treatment programmes is that child sexual abusers experience difficulty in building and maintaining adult relationships. In the author's research 18 of the 21 respondents claimed to have been or were involved in a sexual relationship with an adult woman, 12 had been married or co-habiting at some point in their lives, and two remained in a long-term relationship following their conviction. In some cases the offending had clearly contributed to a breakdown in their relationship. This finding is supported by other research that suggests that abusers have difficulty in relating to adult women (Hammer and Glueck, 1957) and expect isolation and rejection in their sexual adult relationships (Smallbone and Dadds, 1998). In an early study Hammer and Glueck (1957) found that male offenders had a fear of sexual contact with women. Panton (1978) found that abusers tended to be insecure individuals who expected isolation and rejection in their heterosexual contact with others.

The cognitive behavioural treatment approach is based upon the assumption that offenders will be socially isolated individuals incapable of maintaining successful adult relationships. This concept is based upon Finkelhor's (1986) assertion that abusers are more emotionally and sexually congruent with children than with adults. The literature suggests that child sexual abusers as a group may be characterised as socially incompetent, having difficulty in forming the most basic of successful adult relationships (Groth et al., 1982; Marshall and Norgard, 1986). The author's research supports the findings of other work in this area, in that the majority of the respondents (18) did describe considerable ongoing relationship problems that were compounded by the discovery of their offending.

Offenders early lives

In the author's research in-depth interviews were undertaken with the respondents in an attempt to explore their early lives. Respondents recounted difficult, unhappy childhoods: relations with both parents were often characterised by abusive behaviour. Where fathers were present in the respondent's young lives they tended to be either emotionally or physically detached (sometimes for long periods of time) from the family unit. Here fathers were violent, uninterested or both. Relations with mothers were often strained, leaving respondents feeling unloved. Other research has suggested that the parents or carers of a sample of juvenile sex offenders were typically distant and inaccessible, leaving the abusers feeling unloved and uncared for as children (Smith and Israel, 1998). Similarly Bagley (1992) found high levels of parental instability in his sample of convicted child sexual abusers, and Kear-Colwell (1996) asserts that 'most sex offenders come from seriously maladaptive social and family backgrounds and are significantly damaged individuals' (p 262). Some research has pointed to high levels of physical and sexual abuse that can be found in the family histories of child sexual abusers' parents (Lankester and Meyer, 1986).

Evidence from the author's research suggests that respondents experienced problematic relations with others from early childhood to adulthood. It is difficult to validate this finding with reference to other research, given that there has been no thorough attempt to document the life histories of abusers, although Yalom (1975) has suggested, on the basis of his experience as a practitioner, that the origin of relationship problems from this group may lie in experiences of early family life. Research undertaken by Smallbone and Dadds (1998), based upon a small sample of convicted male child sexual abusers, does suggest that poor and abusive relations with parents or carers serves to create problems experienced in adult relationships. The suggestion here is that abusers expect their adult partners to behave in a similar way to their childhood carers – the expectation is that partners will be 'unloving, unresponsive, inconsistent and rejecting' (1998, p 569). These findings have been supported by other research (Ward and Keenan, 1999).

Relationships with parents and experiences of abuse

Respondents in the author's research (Davidson, 2001) spoke frankly about their relationships with their parents. One respondent described his relationship with his father:

> I don't remember having a relationship with him. He was at work, working shifts, and when he *was* there, there was no time for me. My brother and sister were the apple of his eye and got everything they wanted.

Another respondent felt rejected by both parents: 'When we went out I was there because I was supposed to be, not because they [the parents] wanted me.' (R 1.1) The validity of respondents' accounts can be questioned in interview – how far the comments reflect reality is always questionable. It was clear however that the respondents certainly perceived their accounts to be truthful. All of the respondents were interviewed on at least three occasions; many were interviewed at length on five occasions. Their accounts of their early lives proved consistent, and greater detail emerged over time – another respondent described the violence he experienced from his mother:

> A: She's my mother and I love her.
> Q: But how would you describe your relationship?
> A: Well I certainly didn't take it to heart because she's heavy handed. You know as a child I'd get a slap around the ear hole.
> Q: Was she violent?
> A: No . . . just a hard slap around the face or head; it was quite regular but dad never touched us. (R 1.1)

Other respondents spoke of the distance between themselves and their fathers in childhood. It was often the case that these fathers spent long periods of time away from home at work, and had little time for their children when at home:

> My father was a waiter on an ocean liner; I didn't see much of him, he was away most of the time. He didn't take me out, when he wasn't away he'd come in and get drunk and go to

sleep in the chair. I had a lot of contact with him when my mother died last year; we had a relationship in the end, but it was too late. (R 1.6)

The theme of separation from a parent in childhood runs throughout several of the respondent's accounts. In many cases if fathers were not physically absent for long periods of time they were emotionally detached from the family situation, rarely fully participating in family life: indeed a number of the respondents reported feeling fearful of their violent fathers as children.

The quality of paternal relationships among sex offender populations is an area which has been neglected, while there has been a great deal of focus within the psychoanalytic literature upon relations with mothers and mother-figures (Kline, 1987). These studies have been based upon attitudinal testing, and little case-study or life-history research has been undertaken. Another respondent experienced considerable abuse in his relationships with his father:

He [father] had a split personality, Jekyll & Hyde. You would be doing a specific thing and he would see you doing it and thump you ten minutes later. It depended on his mood. Instead of coming over, like you or any other parent would, and saying 'Now don't do that anymore' he would just thump you. He beat me with a strap when he found out I was truanting from school, because of the bullying. (R 1.7)

This respondent experienced considerable ongoing abuse from his father, and described in later interviews how he learnt to avoid or placate his father in order to escape the violence.

Others described their experiences in witnessing domestic violence in the family home. This respondent, whose mother had left the family when he was a small child and who was brought up by his stepmother and father, spoke at length regarding the violence he witnessed before his natural mother left and the emotional abuse he suffered on the part of his stepmother:

A: My mother left when I was small because of my father's behaviour; he'd go out drinking, come back and destroy our home. He would be really violent towards her [mother] for really silly things.

Q: What sort of things?

A: 'Cos she did the potatoes the wrong way or didn't iron a
shirt. I used to hide until it was over. (R 2.3)

This research supports the contention of Smallbone and Dadds
(1998) and Briggs and Kennington (2006) that abusers are likely to
experience problematic relations with parents. The suggestion that
abusers may experience a lifetime of problematic relations with
others, from early childhood into adulthood, constitutes an
important finding. This may offer some explanation: it is possible to
see how, following a lifetime of rejection and problematic relations
with peers, offenders come to associate with children and to feel
happier in their company.

Some commentators have suggested that abusers will probably
have been sexually abused at some point in their childhood. This
follows the contention that a 'cycle' of abuse exists, and that abusers
go on to replicate their experiences in later life (Marshall and Barbaree,
1990; Groth et al., 1982). Approximately half (ten) of the small
sample in the author's research recounted experiences of sexual abuse
as children; it is possible that a larger proportion had experienced
sexual abuse and were unwilling to discuss their experiences, but this
remains unproved. The severity of the abuse experienced varied: three
of the respondents stated that they were sexually abused by a member
of their own family (an older brother and two older cousins)
(Davidson, 2001).

Attitudes towards children

It has been suggested that child sexual abusers have 'distorted'
attitudes towards children, that they sexualise them and objectify
them (Finkelhor, 1986). According to Morrison et al. (1994) this
behaviour may be attributable to the abusers own childhood experiences of sexual abuse. Here the abuser learns that sexual behaviour
between adults and children is acceptable. What of those who did not
(as discussed we cannot assume that all did) experience sexual abuse
as a child? What is the cause of their distortions? The minority of
respondents who claimed to have been sexually abused as children
in the author's research spoke with pain regarding their experiences
– they did not seem to be able to associate the pain they experienced
as victims with that inflicted upon their victims. They were unable to
put themselves in the role of their victim or victims, and had, in a

sense, objectified them. Respondents were asked directly what they liked about children and if they preferred their company to the company of adults. The majority of the respondents stated that they liked children when asked directly, and some felt better able to relate to children than to adults:

A: I really do prefer children to adults.
Q: What do you like about children?
A: Their innocence of the world; there's nothing to worry about, I couldn't hate children. (R 1.12)
A: I like them more [than adults]. They say funny things; they're a lot of fun. Adults aren't fun. (R 1.10)

All except one of the respondents stated that they liked children: the qualities identified consistently were innocence and playfulness, and they also cited the responsibility of adults to teach and pass on knowledge. It is striking that respondents always spoke of children and their behaviour with affection – only one of those interviewed expressed openly negative attitudes towards children. Most were able to identify childlike behaviour, which they admired and with which they, as adults, associated. It could be that respondents were concealing the truth; their actions and thoughts would often demonstrate disregard and on occasions contempt for their victims. This appeared to be a contradiction throughout the research. Respondents would speak of children and their behaviour with warmth and affection and then proceed to describe the abuse they had inflicted upon their victims.

Those who had experienced sexual abuse as children began to talk about the impact of the act/s upon their adult lives, and to think about the impact of their abuse upon their victims. It has been suggested that by perpetrating abuse, abusers are attempting to compensate for an unhappy childhood (Finkelhor, 1986). This, it is suggested, enables abusers to exact some form of revenge.

Research indicates that child sexual abusers often experience troubled childhoods and have difficulty in building relationships throughout their lives; some are emotionally and physically abused by those closest to them. Research does seem to suggest that low self-esteem and social isolation are enduring features in the lives of these offenders, no doubt exacerbated by their conviction and labelling as 'child molester'.

Key child abuse cases: media response and government reaction

Two recent cases involving the abduction, sexual abuse and murder of children by men known to criminal justice agencies to constitute a 'risk' to children have had a far-reaching impact upon the government's policy response to sex offenders, and upon legislation. The cases were reported by the media in detail, from the moment the children disappeared to the subsequent arrest and conviction of the perpetrators: Roy Whiting and Ian Huntley are names that have become inextricably linked in the public subconscious with predatory child abusers.

The Sarah Payne case

The events

On Saturday, 1 July 2000, 8-year-old Sarah Payne wandered away from her siblings following an argument and was promptly abducted by Roy Whiting, a sex offender recently released from prison where he had been serving a sentence for indecent assault on a child, who happened to be passing in his white van. Sarah had been staying with her grandparents in Sussex during the summer holidays. Within a short time her siblings became anxious as they could not find her and promptly informed their grandparents. Several hours later the police launched a search and media campaign, actively enlisting the help of the media in order to find Sarah. It gradually became clear that Sarah had been abducted, and the police began to work with Sarah's parents (Michael and Sara Payne) in appealing to the public for information. There followed an anxious wait and a great deal of media speculation until Sarah's body was found 17 days after her abduction, on 17 July 2000.

The death of Sarah Payne bore many similarities to that of Megan Kanka in the United States. In New Jersey, on 29 July 1994, a warm summer's day, Megan was abducted, raped and murdered by a neighbour, Jesse Timmendequas, a sex offender who had two previous convictions. In 1979 he had been given a suspended sentence for a sexual assault on a 5-year-old, and in 1981 he had been sentenced to six years in custody for sexually assaulting a 7-year-old. The circumstances of the case were similar to that of Sarah Payne. Megan was playing near her home, and was missing for three hours before her mother become anxious. Both children were

1 **July 2000:** Sarah is abducted by Roy Whiting from near her grandparents' home in Sussex. She is reported missing to the police who instigate the search and a media campaign.

2 July: Police begin a fingertip search of the area. In a crackdown on known offenders in the area, Roy Whiting is arrested.

3 July: The first of many emotional televised appeals are made by Michael and Sara Payne for information about Sarah's disappearance. Police arrest another man.

5 July: Roy Whiting and the other man arrested are released on police bail. The police stage an identity parade.

7 July: Using a child similar in appearance to Sarah, a reconstruction of Sarah's last movements is made by the police in an attempt to produce witnesses.

8 July: By Saturday the police had received over 3,500 calls from the public. Roadblocks are set up in the vicinity to seek information from the public about the sighting of a white van and a silver Ford Mondeo. Sarah's brothers and sister make a televised appeal to the public.

13 **July:** The police begin to admit that Sarah may be dead and attempt to prepare her parents and the public for the eventuality. Detective Sergeant Scott admits to what the public had probably suspected; that Sarah 'may not be found safe and well'.

15 **July:** Media coverage of Sarah's parents and siblings making another appeal on the beach from which she disappeared.

17 **July:** Sarah's body is found near Pulborough.

18 **July:** Police confirmation that the body is Sarah's and a murder investigation is launched.

31 **July:** The police arrest Roy Whiting again, and he is later released on police bail.

6 February 2001: The police arrest Roy Whiting for the third time, and he is finally charged with the murder of Sarah Payne.

21 **November:** Judge lifts ban on Roy Whiting's photograph being withheld; the public is introduced to him for the first time.

12 **December:** Following the court case, Roy Whiting is found guilty of abducting and murdering Sarah Payne and is sentenced to life in prison.

Figure 3.2 Sarah Payne: time line of events

Source: Adapted from a BBC website article, 'The Sarah Payne Tragedy', 21 December 2001

visually appealing young girls whose photographs have appeared on countless occasions in international coverage of both their cases and of other similar cases.

Following the murder of her daughter, Megan's mother campaigned for the public disclosure of sex offender's home addresses, and succeeded in forcing the New Jersey state Supreme Court to uphold 'Megan's Law' in 1995. Other states soon followed, and on 17 May 1996 the federal version of the law was enacted. The Jacob Wetterling Crimes Against Children Law was passed in May 1996. This law formed the first part of the federal version of Megan's Law. On 13 September 1996 the 'Megan's Law' notification element of the legislation was passed. All states were given a deadline (September 1997) to pass versions of Megan's Law or risk losing federal aid. Forty-seven states and the District of Columbia passed the legislation. 'Megan's Law' forces states to make information about convicted sex offenders available to the public, but affords discretion in terms of the form the disclosure takes; many states are now publishing offenders' personal information on the internet. States have taken different approaches to public notification: in Oregon sex offenders must display a notice in their windows informing the community about their offence; Washington police officers make home visits to warn communities about sex offenders moving into their areas, and the public in Louisiana has full access to information held by the police about local sex offenders. There are now websites dedicated to providing the American public with detailed information about the location of sex offenders and their risk level. The effectiveness of Megan's Law has been questioned: it seems that a significant proportion of registered offenders (20 per cent) have provided false addresses and disappeared, while others simply offend outside their neighbourhood where they are not closely watched (BBC News, 12 December 2001).

Megan's Law rests upon the principle that parents are entitled to information regarding the whereabouts of dangerous sex offenders in order to take steps to protect their children (Court TV Library, 1995). Under Megan's Law, convicted sex offenders are placed into risk bands. Personal information about 'low-risk' offenders is not disclosed to the public; schools and day care centres are informed about the presence of 'medium-risk' offenders, and the public are informed about the presence and whereabouts of 'high-risk' offenders. In determining risk, the number and nature of offences is considered, as well as victim age and the outcome of any offender therapy. Following the death of Sarah Payne it was not long before the media were calling for the 'naming and shaming' of child sexual abusers living in the UK. A campaign spearheaded by Sara Payne and backed by the *News of the World* sought the introduction of 'Sarah's Law' in the UK. The *News of the World* decided to publish the addresses and photographs of known child sexual abusers – this irresponsible decision prompted vigilante action, crowd protests and the victimisation of innocent people who bore a resemblance to the men in the photographs. The government came under increasing pressure to publish information about sex offenders on the register, and the manner in which 'dangerous' offenders are controlled in the community came sharply into focus, particularly when it became apparent that Roy Whiting had been on the sex offenders register since 1995. The vigilante attacks provoked by the *News of the World* provided the government with a good basis on which to deny the demand of the Payne family and the media to introduce Sarah's Law, and to disclose information about sex offenders in the community.

The BBC reported the government's position immediately following the death of Sarah Payne:

> The government actively considered the matter and took advice from the agencies most closely involved in protecting the public from sex offenders, namely the police and probation services, and from children's charities. . . . The government concluded that granting such access was likely to hinder rather than help measures to protect children.
>
> (Gould, 2001)

The National Probation Service supported the government, with Harry Fletcher (then Assistant General Secretary of the National Association of Probation Officers) claiming that Sarah's Law would not work as sex offenders would be driven underground and would not register as freely (there is currently a 97 per cent compliance rate) and that the actions of the *News of the World* led to public violence. Fletcher set the scene for increasingly punitive legislation and extreme measures of control when he said that effective risk management and behavioural control were key (Hall, *Guardian*, 13 December 2001). Although Sarah's Law was not introduced, the Sarah Payne case led to a review of risk assessment and management of sex offenders in the community and informed the Sexual Offences Act 2003.

The disclosure debate in the UK continues: Gerry Sutcliffe, a Junior Minister, has recently visited New Jersey (July 2006) on behalf of the Home Office to establish if Megan's Law could be implemented in the UK. Although Sutcliffe expressed reservations regarding the adoption of the law, he stated that any changes in the British approach would include three aspects:

1   Reinforced Multi-Agency Panel Protection Arrangements (MAPPA);
2   Sex offender treatment;
3   Controlled information in communities.

(BBC News website, 23 July 2006)

The third element – 'controlled information in communities' – suggests that the government may stop short of community disclosure, but may target disclosure to specific community groups such as parents.[2] The influence of the media upon the government was never more apparent than when Sutcliffe's visit to the United States was announced in the *News of the World*. This led to heated exchanges in Parliament, where the Prime Minister (through his official spokesman) was asked if he agreed with the accusation made by a senior police officer that the government had been 'blackmailed' by the *News of the World*. The Prime Minister's Official Spokesman (PMOS) said that everyone needed to:

> recognise that there was a balance to be struck between what was a genuine ongoing concern in many local communities around the country and the need to give the public information which reassured them while avoiding vigilantism. This was the essential balance. The Home Secretary had announced two perfectly sensible things. One, that paedophiles would not be housed in hostels near schools. Two, that Gerry Sutcliffe would travel to the US to study 10 years worth of experience of Megan's Law. Both of these were important and were not something we were rushing into. We were taking our time to study whether we could do more to get that balance right. This was a responsible thing for a government to do given that it was a subject of genuine concern in communities.

2   This measure is now proposed under recent Home Office policy (2007).

The PMOS was then asked if ministers had met with News International; a meeting was not denied, and he was pressed regarding the decision to make the announcement via the newspaper and not in Parliament. A rather harassed PMOS responded that this seemed reasonable given that the newspaper had first raised the issue. It is clear from the debate that the government had been discussing both the planned trip and possible measures to control sex offenders with the *News of the World* well in advance of informing Parliament. This could be viewed as an attempt to assuage public unrest and quell continued pressure to 'name and shame' sex offenders. It may only be a question of time before sex offenders' locations and personal details are made public in the UK (Downing Street Says Archives, 2006).

The Soham murders

The impact of the Sarah Payne case upon policy and legislation regarding the control and treatment of sex offenders has been far-reaching, and may have forced the government into an uneasy compromise with a tabloid newspaper that had provoked vigilante riots and public disorder by publishing the photographs of 50 known sex offenders. The abduction and murder of two children in Soham in August 2002 by Ian Huntley, a person known to two police forces (Humberside and Lincolnshire) and against whom previous allegations of sexual abuse had been made, led the media and the public to further question the competence of the Home Office and its criminal justice agencies in tracking and monitoring known sex offenders. Not only was Huntley known to the police, he was also working as a school caretaker and had unlimited access to children on a daily basis.

The events

The circumstances surrounding the death of Holly Wells and Jessica Chapman are remarkably similar to those surrounding the death of Sarah Payne and Megan Kanka in the United States. On a warm Sunday evening in Soham, Cambridgeshire, in August 2002, the two 10-year-old girls decided to leave their parents barbecue and go for a walk. The adults were holding a barbecue in the garden and did not realise that the girls had left the house for some time. Jessica Chapman's last recorded use of her mobile phone was at 6.46 pm. Jessica and Holly encountered Ian Huntley, a caretaker at their school, that evening and were drawn into his house. He murdered them and buried their bodies the next day. The story began as did Sarah Payne's; the missing children reported, the involvement of the police and the siege of Soham by the media, the tense wait for news, the family pleas for information, the endless publication of images of the children, and finally the revelation that the school caretaker, a man known in the community, was responsible for their murder, possibly aided in concealing the crime by a woman known to the girls, Maxine Carr.

Media criticism of the police was considerable following the arrest and conviction of Ian Huntley. It was becoming clear that a number of sexual abuse allegations had been made to two police forces (Humberside and Lincolnshire), and that had Cambridgeshire Police conducted the most basic of searches before clearing Huntley to work in the school they would have discovered this fact. The school had requested the standard child protection clearance from the police. BBC News commented: 'A detective who took no action against Ian Huntley over three allegations of underage sex admitted his decisions would have been "totally different" if he had linked all of the accusations' (19 December 2003).

Social services and the CPS were also held to account for a failure to pick up on Huntley's past and to effectively prosecute a previous allegation. BBC News commented on the failure of social services to act upon information about allegations involving Huntley having sex with underage girls:

> Social services dealing with Soham killer Ian Huntley failed to act on allegations he had sexual relations with 11 girls before 2001. A report details cases of girls dealt with by North-East Lincolnshire Social Services when Huntley was living in the Grimsby area in the mid-1990s. Sir Christopher Kelly, who conducted the review, said opportunities had been missed by social workers and police. He said the killer's history 'should have rung significant warning bells'.
>
> (19 December 2003)

It really could not have looked worse for the government, the Home Office and its agencies – they were still recovering from the fallout of the Sarah Payne case, and the media made sure that the public were fully apprised of this. An inquiry was set up into the conduct of the Soham case, chaired by Sir Michael Bichard, Rector of the London

4 August 2002: The last photograph of Holly Wells and Jessica Chapman is taken – the clock behind them reads 17.04. The girls go for a walk and are last sighted at 18.30 by a neighbour. At 20.30 their parents realise they have left the house.

5 August: The police and volunteer search begins; the police enlist the help of the media and launch a public appeal for information.

7 August: The girls' parents make the first of many emotional appeals for information at a press conference.

8 August: The police release CCTV footage of Jessica and Holly in the car park of a local sports centre; a further appeal for information is made. The police thought that the girls were still alive based on information from criminal profilers (the girls had been dead since Sunday, 4 August).

10 August: A reconstruction of the girls' last movements is made; Soham is now besieged by the media.

15 August: The Metropolitan Police are asked to review the practice of Cambridgeshire police in searching for the girls.

17 August: Police search the home of a Soham man and woman and the girls' school. A 28-year-old man is arrested on suspicion of abduction and murder, and a 25-year-old woman is arrested on suspicion of murder. Police confirm that two bodies have been found near an airbase at Mildenhall in Suffolk.

18 August: Police are granted an extra 36 hours to question 28-year-old Ian Huntley and his girlfriend Maxine Carr, 25. The bodies are removed for examination; police confirm that they are almost certain that the bodies are the remains of Holly and Jessica.

20 August: Ian Huntley is charged with the murder of Jessica Chapman and Holly Wells.

16 April 2003: Huntley pleads not guilty to murder and Maxine Carr pleads not guilty to conspiring to pervert the course of justice.

3 November: The trial of Huntley and Carr begins at the Central Criminal Court, London.

17 December: Huntley found guilty of murder and Carr found guilty of conspiracy.

Figure 3.3 Soham: time line of events

Source: Adapted from a BBC News website article, 18 August 2002, 3 November 2004

Institute and a former Permanent Secretary at the Department for Education and Employment. The Bichard Inquiry reported to the Home Secretary on 14 June 2004 and its report was published on 22 June 2004. During the inquiry in March 2004 the *Daily Mail* suggested: 'Second Force Had Report on Huntley' – and that a request to the Criminal Records Bureau clearance would have revealed that allegations of sexual abuse had been made against Huntley; the report suggests that Cambridgeshire Police probably did not. (*Daily Mail*, 30 March 2004)

Once the Bichard Inquiry began and the nature of Ian Huntley's previous offending behaviour became clear, the media criticism was endless: the *Sun* suggested that the police could have prevented the offence (*Sun*, 28 June 2004).

Commenting more recently, *The Times* said:

> Huntley: A History of Violence (. . .) Had he been convicted, he would have been kept under close supervision. But, instead, he was approved to work as a school caretaker and murdered Holly Wells and Jessica Chapman in August 2002. Police were aware that he had had a number of sexual relationships with underage girls and that he was the subject of nine allegations of rape and indecent assault. He had been officially identified as a serial sex attacker.
>
> (27 November 2006)

The Bichard Inquiry agreed, and was most damming in its criticism of Humberside Police for their failure to maintain adequate intelligence (2004, p 77); failure to share information effectively (2004, p 84) and failure to identify a clear crime pattern in Huntley's previous behaviour (2004, p 88). Cambridgeshire Police were criticised for the manner in which the investigation was conducted. Two key recommendations arising from the Bichard Inquiry were that a national IT system for police intelligence should be set up in England and Wales as soon as possible, and that a registration scheme should operate for all those working in close proximity to children – this could possibly take the form of a credit card listing previous employment and any offence allegations that would have to be updated on a regular basis. Bichard also recommended measures for strengthening vetting procedures and the handling of child sexual abuse allegations (Bichard Inquiry Report, 2004). The government have responded to the recommendations made in the Bichard Report

– in a letter from the Secretary of State to the Home Department (Charles Clarke) the government accepts the recommendations and describes progress made in setting up an IT police system, IMPACT (Information, Management, Prioritisation, Analysis and Tasking System), which will be completed in 2007, and in responding to the other recommendations made (11 January 2005). An Independent Barring Board was also established in the Safeguarding Vulnerable Groups Act 2006. One of the Board's functions will be to maintain a comprehensive and up-to-date list of adults barred from working with children.

Newspaper response to the perpetrators

The media response to the Sarah Payne and Soham cases has been considerable. A search suggests that the number of articles containing information about the Sarah Payne case is as follows: *Sun*, 1,632; *Mirror*, 90; *Daily Mail*, 1,286; *Guardian*, 537 and *The Times*, 139 articles. The number of articles on the Soham case were as follows: *Sun*, 531; *Mirror*, over 100 articles; *Daily Mail*, 194; *Guardian*, 868 and *The Times*, 522 articles. A current case involving the abduction of a child from a holiday resort in Portugal has attracted a great deal of UK and international media attention: although there is no evidence that the child has been taken by a child abuser at present, the series of events surrounding the abduction and its subsequent discovery are remarkably similar to events surrounding the Soham and Sarah Payne cases. Madeleine McCann, aged four, disappeared from her parents' villa on the evening of 3 May 2007. Police fear that she may have been abducted by a sex offender ring or a lone sex offender. During a four-week period from the date of Madeleine McCann's abduction the *Daily Mail* ran 63 articles on the case. The *Sun* included 88 articles on the case, claiming that Portugal is a haven for sex offenders (an unfounded claim based only on the absence of a sex offenders register in the country) (10 May 2007). The *Guardian* ran nine articles, and five articles were featured in *The Times*. Tabloid newspaper and television media attention received by the case in a short time period is unprecedented. Large rewards have been offered for the safe return of Madeleine; the McCann's were granted an audience with the Pope, and were flown to Rome via private jet; a fund has been set up with substantial donations to extend the hunt for the missing girl. While everyone hopes for the safe return of Madeleine, the case seems to have become the focal point for parents' collective fear regarding the potential abduction of their children by sex offenders. Many children are listed as missing, but few cases attract such attention and media focus – the European Federation for Missing and Sexually Exploited Children (2007, www.europeanfederation-children.org/) claim that thousands of children are reported missing on a daily basis, while the National Center for Missing and Exploited Children claims that a child goes missing every 40 seconds in the United States (www.missingkids.com).

If child sexual abusers have become the media personification of 'evil', none could be more evil than Roy Whiting and Ian Huntley, whose physical characteristics and every action have been taken as confirming this fact. The *Sun* called Whiting a 'sex beast' (6 August 2002) and another story discussing Whiting's childhood described him as a 'monster' (13 December 2001). Following Whiting's conviction the *Sun* headline read: 'Forget About Rights For Evil Pervs Like Whiting'. Descriptions of Huntley have been similar. The *Sun*, commenting on his cowardice in a failed hunger strike in prison, said: 'Evil Huntley Hasn't the Guts to Starve Himself' (15 December 2004). In reporting the claims of two other victims, the *Sun* described Huntley as '*vile*', stating 'We will Cheer when vile Huntley Dies in his Cell' (29 November 2004). Greer and Jewkes (2005) have commented that intense media focus around isolated, extreme crimes serves to create and reinforce commonly held social beliefs about a group of offenders. Attention becomes directed at all registered sex offenders, many of whom will have committed substantially less serious offences. In this way sex offenders as a group have become demonised. Greer and Jewkes point to the hypocrisy of a society which condones the sexualisation of young children appearing in fashion magazines and on television, but condemns the sexual abuse of children and young people. They suggest that society is perhaps attempting to 'mitigate a feeling of complicity' (2005, p 22) through moral outrage expressed in the media and through the introduction of increasingly harsher penalties for sex offenders convicted of abusing children. The vilification of Roy Whiting and Ian Huntley for what were heinous crimes against children has refocused public attention upon the 'What is to be done with the sex offenders?' debate. The revelations regarding the failure to protect the community from known sexual 'predators' and the ensuing criticism led to pressure to introduce legislation permitting the disclosure of sex offenders' locations and to the Bichard Inquiry, which has recommended the development of a coherent police IT system.

Key chapter themes

• More is known about male child sexual abusers than is known about female offenders; perpetrators tend to be male and victims tend to be female. There appears to be no link with social class or ethnicity.

• Psychology has made the greatest contribution to understanding motivations and the cognitive behavioural theoretical approach underpins offender treatment in the UK.

• Research indicates that child sexual abusers are likely to have low self-esteem; be socially isolated; experience difficulty in building and maintaining adult relationships; and may have experienced abuse as children.

• Two cases involving the abduction and murder of children (Sarah Payne, Holly Wells and Jessica Chapman) have had a far-reaching impact upon government policy and on moves to control sex offenders in the community. Media representation of the offences and the perpetrators has played a key role in this process.

References

Aarens, M, Roizen, J, Roizen, R, Room, R, Schneberk, D and Wingard, D, *Alcohol, Casualties and Crime*, 1977, Berkeley: Research Group

Abel, G C and Becker, J V, 'The treatment of child molesters', 1984, Treatment Manual, unpublished

Abel, G C and Becker, J V, 'Self reported sex crimes of non-incarcerated paraphilliacs', *Journal of Interpersonal Violence*, 2(6) (1987), pp 3–25

Abel, G C, Cunningham-Rathner, J, Becker, J V and McHugh, J, 'Motivating sex offenders for treatment', in Finkelhor (ed), *A Sourcebook on Child Sexual Abuse*, 1983, California: Sage

Almond, L, Canter, D and Salfati, G, 'Youths who sexually harm: A multivariate model of characteristics', *Journal of Sexual Aggression*, 12(2) (July 2006), pp 97–114

American Humane Association, *National Study on Child Neglect and Associated Abuse Reporting*, 1981, Colorado: Sage

Bagley, C, 'Characteristics of 60 children and adolescents with a history of sexual assault against others: Evidence from a comparative study', *Journal of Forensic Psychiatry*, 3(2) (1992), pp 212–20

Baker, A and Duncan, S, 'Child sexual abuse: A study of prevalence in Great Britain', *Child Abuse and Neglect*, 9 (1985), pp 457–67

Barker, M and Morgan, R, *Sex Offenders: A Framework for the Evaluation of Community Based Treatment*, 1993, London: Home Office

Barnett, S, Corder, F and Jehu, D, 'Group treatment for women sex offenders against children', *Groupwork*, 3(2) (1990), pp 191–203

Becker, J V and Kaplan, L, 'The assessment of adolescent sex offenders', *Advances in Behavioural Assessment of Children and Families*, 4 (1988), pp 97–118

Beckett, R C, Beech, A, Fisher, D and Fordham, A S, *Community Based Treatment for Sex Offenders: An Evaluation of Seven Treatment Programmes*, 1994, London: Home Office

Berlin, F S and Hopkins, J, 'Sexual deviation syndromes', *Medical Coyle, G S Journal*, 149 (1981), pp 119–25

Bichard Inquiry Report, 2004, accessed January 2007, www.bichardinquiry. org.uk/report/

Bowlby, J, *Attachment and Loss*, Vol 2, 1973, New York: Basic Books

Briggs, D and Kennington, R, *Managing Men Who Sexually Abuse*, 2006, London: Jessica Kingsley

Carter, B J, *Who's to Blame? Child Sexual Abuse and Non-Offending Mothers*, 1999, Toronto: University of Toronto Press

Clark, R W, *Freud: The Man and the Cause*, 1982, London: Granada

Clarke, C, 'Bichard Inquiry: Implementation of recommendations', Letter from Secretary of State to the Home Department, 2005, accessed November 2006, www.bichardinquiry.org.uk/pdf/Bichard-Final_WMS-11Jan04.pdf

Coulborn-Faller, K, 'Sex offenders and their victims', 1993, NSPCC conference proceedings

Court TV Library, 'New Jersey v Timmendequas', 1995, accessed November 2006, www.courttv.com/archive/casefiles/verdicts/kanka.html

Davidson, J, 'The context and practice of community treatment programmes for convicted child sexual abusers in England and Wales', unpublished PhD thesis, 2001, London School of Economics and Political Science

Davidson, J, 'Victims speak: Comparing child sexual abusers and their victims accounts of offence circumstance', *Journal of Victims and Offenders*, 1 (2005), pp 159–74

Davidson, J, 'Current practice and research into internet sex offending', 2007, Risk Management Authority (Scotland), accessed May 2007, www.rmascotland.gov.uk/currentprojects.aspx

Davidson, J and Martellozzo, E, 'Protecting children in cyberspace', in Letherby, G, Birch, P, Cain, M and Williams, K (eds), *Sex as Crime* (forthcoming, March 2008), London: Willan Publishing

De Young, M, *Sexual Victimisation of Children*, 1982, New York: McFarland

Downing Street Says, 'Paedophiles and *News of the World*', 20 June 2006, accessed June 2006, www.downingstreetsays.org/archives/002817.html

Elliot, M, *The Ultimate Taboo*, 1993, London: Longman

Elliot, M, Browne, K and Kilcoyne, J, 'Child sexual abuse prevention: What offenders tell us', *Child Abuse and Neglect*, 19 (1995), pp 579–94

European Federation for Missing and Sexually Exploited Children 2007, accessed February 2007, www.europeanfederation-children.org/

Fagan, J and Wexler, S, 'Explanations of sexual assault amongst violent delinquents', *Journal of Adolescent Research*, 3(2) (1988), pp 363–85

Faller, K C, *Understanding Child Sexual Maltreatment*, 1990, California: Sage

Finkelhor, D, *Sexually Victimised Children*, 1979, New York: Free Press

Finkelhor, D, *Child Sexual Abuse: New Theory and Research*, 1984, New York: Free Press

Finkelhor, D and Russell, D, 'Women as perpetrators', in Finkelhor, D, *Child Sexual Abuse: New Theory and Research*, 1984, New York: Free Press, pp 171–87

Fisher, D, 'Sex offenders: who are they, why are they?' in Morrison, T, Erooga, M and Beckett, R (eds), *Sexual Offending against Children: Assessment and Treatment of Male Abusers*, 1994, London: Routledge

Freud, S, *Heredity and the Etiology of the Neurosis*, standard edition, 1896, pp 141–61

Freud, S, *Introductory Lectures on Psycho-analysis*, 9th edn (originally published 1922), 1952, London: Allen & Unwin

Fromouth, M E, 'The long-term psychological impact of childhood sexual abuse', unpublished paper, 1983, Auburn University, Auburn, Alabama

Garcia, E E, 'Freud's seduction theory', *Psychoanalytic Study of the Child*, 42 (1987), pp 443–68

Gillan, A, 'Race to save new victims of child pornography', *Guardian*, 4 November 2003

Gorry, P, 'Incest: the offence and police investigation', in La Fontaine, J, *Child Sexual Abuse*, 1988, ESRC Research Briefing, 1/88

Gould, P, 'Protecting children from paedophiles', BBC News, 12 December 2001, http://news.bbc.co.uk/1/england/1672022.stm

Graves, R B, Openshaw, K, Ascione, F and Ericksen, S, 'Demographic and parental characteristics of youthful sex offenders', *International Journal of Offender Therapy and Comparative Criminology*, 40(4) (1996), pp 300–17

Greer, C and Jewkes, Y, 'Extremes of otherness: Media images of social exclusion', in *Social Justice*, special edition on 'Emerging imaginaries of regulation, control and oppression', 32(1) (2005), pp 20–31

Groth, N A, Longo, R E and McFadin, J B, 'Undetected recidivism in rapists and child molesters', *Crime and Delinquency*, 28 (1982), pp 450–8

Gudjonsson, G, 'The revised Gudjonsson blame attribution inventory', *Personal Individual Differences*, 10(1) (1987), pp 67–70

Gudjonsson, G, 'Self deception and other deception in forensic assessment', *Personal Individual Differences*, 11(3) (1990), pp 219–25

Gudjonsson, G, 'The attribution of blame and type of crime committed: Transcultural validation', *Journal of Forensic Science Society*, 31(3) (1991), pp 349–52

Hall, S, 'Argument rages over Sarah's law – why parents' key demand is rejected by police', *Guardian Unlimited*, 13 December 2001

Hammer, R F and Gleuck, B C, 'Psycho-dynamic patterns in sex offenders: A four factor theory', *Psychiatric Quarterly*, 31 (1957), pp 325–45

Herman, J and Herschman, L, 'Father and daughter incest', *Journal of Women, Culture and Society*, 2 (1977), pp 735–56

Hitschmann, E, *Freud's Theories of the Neuroses*, 1921, London: Kegan Paul

Home Office, 'Statistical Bulletin sentencing statistics', 2005, accessed 21 February 2007, England & Wales RDS NOMS, www.homeoffice.gov.uk

Hucker, S J and Bain, J, 'Androgenic hormones and sexual assault', in Marshall, W L, Laws, D R and Barbaree, H E (eds), *Handbook of Sexual Assault*, 1990, New York: Plenum

Hutton, L and Whyte, B, 'Children and young people with harmful sexual behaviours: First analysis of data from a Scottish sample', *Journal of Sexual Aggression*, 12(2) (July 2006), pp 115–25

Kaplan, M S, 'The impact of parolees perceptions of confidentiality on the reporting of their urges to interact sexually with children', in Morrison, T, Erooga, M and Beckett, R (eds), *Sexual Offending Against Children*, 1985, London: Routledge

Kear-Colwell, J, 'Guest editorial: A personal position on the treatment of individuals who commit sexual offences', *International Journal of Offender Therapy and Comparative Criminology*, 40(4) (1996), pp 259–62

Kelly, L, *Surviving Sexual Violence*, 1988, Oxford: Blackwell

Kelly, L, Regan, L and Burton, S, 'An exploratory study of the prevalence of sexual abuse in a sample of 16-31 year olds', 1991, North London University, Child Abuse Studies Unit, London: PNL

Kline, P, 'Psychoanalysis and crime', in McGurk, B, Thornton, D and Williams, M, *Applying Psychology to Imprisonment: Theory and Practice*, 1987, London: HMSO

Krone, T, 'A typology of online child pornography offending', *Trends and Issues in Crime and Criminal Justice*, 279 (2004), Canberra: Australian Institute of Criminology

La Fontaine, J, 'Child sexual abuse', 1988, ESRC Research Briefing, London: ESRC

Langevin, R, 'Sexual anomalies and the brain', in Marshall, W, Laws, D R and Barbaree, H R (eds), *Handbook of Sexual Assault: Issues, Theories and Treatment of the Offender*, 1990, New York: Plenum

Lankester, D and Meyer, B, 'Relationship of family structure to sex offender behaviour', unpublished paper presented at the First National Conference on Juvenile Sexual Offending, 1986, Minneapolis, MN

Lanyon, R L, 'Theories of sex offending', in Howells, C R (ed), *Clinical Approaches to Sex Offenders and their Victims*, 1991, Chichester: J Wiley

LaRue, J, 'When beauty is the beast', Concerned Women for America website, 2006, accessed 10 November 2006, www.cwfa.org/articledisplay. asp?id=10763&department=legal&categoryid=pornography

Laws, D R, and Marshall, W L, 'A conditioning theory of the etiology maintenance of deviant sexual preference and behaviour', in Marshall, W, Laws, D R and Barbaree, H R (eds), *Handbook of Sexual Assault: Issues, Theories and Treatment of the Offender*, 1990, New York: Plenum

Madden, M F and Wrench, D F, 'Significant findings in child abuse research', *Victimology*, 2 (1977), pp 196–224

Marshall, W L, 'Assessment, treatment and theorizing about sex offenders: Developments over the last twenty years and future directions', *Criminal Justice and Behaviour*, 23 (1996), pp 162–99

Marshall, W L and Barbaree, H E, 'An integrated theory of the etiology of sexual offending' in Marshall, W, Laws, D R and Barbaree, H R (eds), *Handbook of Sexual Assault: Issues, Theories and Treatment of the Offender*, 1990, New York: Plenum

Marshall, W L and Norgard, K E, *Child Abuse and Neglect: Sharing Responsibility*, 1983, New York: J Wiley.

Masson, J M, *The Assault on Truth: Freud's Suppression of the Seduction Theory*, 1984, New York: Farrar, Strauss and Giroux

Masson, J M (ed), *The Complete Letters of Sigmund Freud to Wilhelm Fliess, 1887–1904*, 1985, Cambridge: Harvard University Press

Matthews, R, *Female Sexual Offenders: An Exploratory Study*, 1989, Orwell, VT: Safer Society Press

Morrison, T, Erooga, M and Beckett, R (eds), *Sexual Offending Against Children: Assessment and Treatment of Male Abusers*, 1994, London: Routledge

Moultrie, D, 'Adolescents convicted of possession of abuse images of children: A new type of adolescent sex offender?', *Journal of Sexual Aggression*, 12(2) (July 2006), pp 165–74

Mrazek, P B and Kemp, C H, *Sexually Abused Children and their Families*, 1981, Oxford: Pergamon

Nash, C L and West, D J, 'Sexual molestation of young girls: A retrospective study', in West, D J (ed), *Sexual Victimisation*, 1985, Aldershot: Gower

National Center for Missing and Exploited Children, accessed January 2007, www.missingkids.com

Northern Ireland Research Team, *Child Sexual Abuse in Northern Ireland*, 1991, Belfast: Greystone

O'Callaghan, D and Print, B, 'Adolescent sexual abusers: Research assessment and treatment', in Morrison, T, Erooga, M and Beckett, R, *Sexual Offending Against Children*, 1994, London: Routledge

Oliver, D, *A Comparison of the Personality Characteristics of Adolescent Sex Offenders and other Adolescent Offenders*, 1993, California: Sage

Peplau, L A and Perlman, D, *Loneliness: A Sourcebook of Current Theory, Research and Therapy*, 1982, New York: John Wiley

Pithers, W D, 'Empathy: Definition, enhancement, and relevance to the treatment of sexual abusers', *Journal of Interpersonal Violence*, 14(3) (1999), pp 257–84

Quayle, E and Taylor, M, 'Model of problematic internet use in people with a sexual interest in children', *Cyberpsychology and Behaviour*, 6(1) (2003), pp 93–106

Rada, R, Laws, D and Kellner, R, 'Plasma testosterone levels in the rapist', *Psychosomatic Medicine*, 38(4) (1976), pp 257–68

Rook, K S, 'The functions of social bonds: Perspectives on research from social support, loneliness and social isolation', in Sarason, I G and Sarason, B R (eds), *Social Support, Theory, Research and Applications*, 1985, Holland: Martinus Nijjhoff

Rush, F, 'The sexual abuse of children: The feminist point of view', in Connell, N and Wilson, C, *Rape: The First Sourcebook for Women*, 1974, London: Plume

Salter, A, *Treating Child Sex Offenders and Victims: A Practical Guide*, 1988, California: Sage

'The Sarah Payne tragedy', BBC News, 21 December 2001, accessed January 2007, http://news.bbc.co.uk/1/hi/england/17035.stm

Smallbone, S W and Dadds, M R, 'Childhood attachment and adult attachment in incarcerated adult male sex offenders', *Journal of Interpersonal Violence*, 13(5) (1998), pp 555–73

Smith, H and Israel, E, 'Sibling incest: A study of the dynamics of 25 cases', *Child Abuse and Neglect*, 2 (1987), pp 98–110

Smith, W R, 'Delinquency and abuse amongst juvenile sex offenders', *Journal of Interpersonal Violence*, 3(4) (1988), pp 379–90

Sparks, C, *The Discovery of Animal Behaviour*, 1982, London: Macmillan

Taylor, M, Holland, G and Quayle, E, 'Typology of paedophile picture collections', *The Police Journal*, 74(2) (2001), pp 97–107

Walters, D R, *Physical and Sexual Abuse of Children: Causes and Treatment*, 1975, Bloomington: Indiana Press

Ward, T and Keenan, T, 'Child molesters: Implicit theories', *Journal of Interpersonal Violence*, 14(8) (1999), pp 821–38

Warren, J and Hislop, J, 'Practical aspects of rape investigation: A multidisciplinary approach', in Hazelwood, R and Wolbert Burges, A, *The Female Sexual Offender*, cited at Concerned Women For America

Website, Chief Counsel, 2006, accessed May 2007, www.cwfa.org/article display.asp?id=10763&department=LEGAL&categoryid=pornography

Weinrott, M R and Saylor, M, 'Self report of crimes committed by sex offenders', *Journal of Interpersonal Violence*, 6(3) (1991), pp 286–300

Weldon, E V, 'Mother, madonna, whore: The idealisation and denegration of motherhood', 1988, London: Free Association Press

Wolf, S, 'A multi-factor model of deviant sexuality', in Morrison, T, Erooga, M and Beckett, R, *Sexual Offending Against Children*, 1984, London: Routledge. Paper presented at Third International Conference on Victimology, 1984, Lisbon

Wortley, R and Smallbone, S, 'Child pornography on the internet', 2006, US Department of Justice, Office of Community Orientated Policing Services, www.cops.usdoj.gov/mime/open.pdf?Item=1729

Wyre, R, 'No excuse for child porn', *Community Care*, 1489 (2003), pp 38–40

Chapter 4

Sentencing child sexual abusers and the legislative framework

This chapter seeks to:

- Examine the legislative framework of sentencing for child sexual abusers in England and Wales, focusing upon advice produced by the Sentencing Advisory Panel and the Crown Prosecution Service.

- Explore sentencing trends and practice for sex offenders in England and Wales and newspaper response to sentencing practice.

- Explore international approaches to the sentencing of sex offenders.

Sentencing guidance and the Sexual Offences Act 2003

The Sexual Offences Act 2003 came into force on 1 May 2004 and replaces the Sexual Offences Act 1956. The Sentencing Advisory Panel (SAP) recommend that the presiding principles of the Criminal Justice Act (CJA) 2003 should be the key determinant in sentencing sex offenders: the 'culpability' of the offender and the 'harm' caused to the victim. Harm and potential risk to society should also be considered. The nature of the harm caused to victims is listed under several headings:

1   Violation of the victim's sexual autonomy – this really addresses victim impact and cases are considered more serious where abuse occurs within a family context or is perpetrated by those in a position of trust.

2 Exploitation of a vulnerable victim – including children and those with a mental disorder.

3 Embarrassment, distress or humiliation of the victim – the description is rather vague but this refers to degrees of humiliation and distress, it is not necessarily linked to the offence category. For example, an internet-related offence might cause extreme humiliation if images which form a permanent record are posted on the internet.

4 Infringement of standards of socially acceptable behaviour – the examples cited here are bestiality and necrophilia, although how these categories of offence might impinge directly upon the victims is questionable.

(Sentencing Advisory Panel, 2006, p 6)

Specifically, sentencers are advised by the SAP to consider: offender culpability; the nature of the sexual activity; the harm caused to the victim; the age and degree of vulnerability of the victim and the age gap between the child and the offender when sentencing offenders committing sexual offences against children (SAP, 2006a). Offender culpability is considered to be linked to degree of pre-meditation or offence planning – impulsive offending is not considered as serious.

Victim age is considered an important and potentially aggravating factor, particularly where a considerable age gap exists between the perpetrator and the child. The principle here is that the younger the child victim and the greater the age gap, the more severe the sentence should be. Offences involving the rape and penetration of a child under 13 now carry the maximum life penalty under the Sexual Offences Act 2003 – the fact that a victim is under 13 should indicate a higher starting point for the sentence. However, the SAP also warns that the youth and mental maturity of the offender should be taken into account.

The new offence of 'sexual assault' carries a maximum penalty of 14 years where the victim is a child under 13, and covers all forms of sexual touching. This replaces the 'indecent assault' category introduced under the Sexual Offences Act 1956. This new category now covers offences that would have fallen at the lower end of the 'indecent assault' category, responding to considerable criticism by commentators such as Ashworth (1999), who claimed that the term 'indecent assault' encompassed many different types of sexual offence, from kissing a child in a sexual manner to touching a child's genitals or enforced oral sex. There clearly is a great deal of difference between the two categories of crime in terms of seriousness and impact upon the victim. Ashworth argued that two categories of indecent assault should exist in English law to differentiate between relatively minor and more serious offences: 'this suggests that there is a strong argument for having two grades of indecent assault in English law, or for moving some of the more serious forms of the crime into a broadened crime of rape or "serious sexual assault"' (1999, p 362).

SAP now advise that the seriousness of the offending should guide the use of the 'sexual assault' category in sentencing. How far this guidance will dissuade sentencers from employing the offence category as a 'catch all' category, as was the case with 'indecent assault', remains to be seen. The manner in which offences are categorised has a direct bearing upon the sentencing of offenders. A good example is provided by the old 'indecent assault' category: the manner in which a number of different types of sexual offence were categorised as indecent assault had implications for the way in which offenders were sentenced. In research exploring the effectiveness of a community sex offender treatment programme undertaken by the author prior to the introduction of the Sexual Offences Act 2003, the majority of respondents in the small group who underwent the treatment programme had been convicted of 'indecent assault' (18 of 21) under the 1956 Sexual Offences Act. The nature of their offending ranged from touching children in passing in a public place to systematic, enforced oral sex. The sentence received was the same for those committing relatively minor offences (non-contact) as it was for those committing more serious (contact) offences.

Three other groups of offences involving the sexual abuse of children, which are described by the SAP as 'ostensibly consensual' (2006b, p 46; Sexual Offences Act 2003, Part 3A) include: 'child sex offences' involving children under 16 (but over 13) (this may include arranging an offence); 'familial child sex offences', committed mainly by members of the child's household; and 'abuse of a position of trust',[1] which includes those in a position of authority, a concept first introduced to English law under the Sexual Offences (Amendment) Act 2000. The guidance states that a reasonable defence here is that the child's true age was not known and was effectively concealed.

---

1   The Sexual Offences Act 2003 raises the age of consent to under 18 in the 'abuse of a position of trust' category.

However, where offending is committed by a family member this is considered to be an aggravating factor, and SAP advise that the starting point for sentencing should be between 25 per cent and 50 per cent higher than for other child sexual offences. Such offending is considered more serious as it is sometimes sustained and perpetrated by someone from whom the child could have expected protection and support. The 'familial child sex offences' category replaces the old category of 'incest', which was incorporated into English law by the Punishment of Incest Act 1908. This offence, as applied to children, included sexual intercourse (vaginal intercourse) by any male blood relative. Ashworth (1999), commenting prior to the Sexual Offences Act 2004, suggested that 'incest' should not be restricted to vaginal intercourse and should cover other forms of sexual abuse; the category now includes all forms of contact and non-contact child sexual abuse.

Guidance suggests that where an offence category covers a wide range of sexual behaviour, as many categories have in the past and continue to do so, sentencers should consider the degree of harm caused to the victim. Cases where an 'abuse of trust' (following the Sexual Offences (Amendment) Act 2000) is involved are to be viewed more seriously. For example, in an appeal against sentence severity in the case of *R v Hubbard* (which involved a school teacher who had sexually abused a 15-year-old student), the Court of Appeal held that the degree of sexual exploitation and the nature of the offending were secondary issues compared to 'position of trust' ([2002] 2 Cr App R (S) 473).

A new range of 'exploitation' offences are introduced in the Sexual Offences Act 2003: these include indecent photographs of children and the abuse of children through pornography and prostitution. Similar principles apply in determining offence seriousness. Offender culpability is a key issue – for example, evidence of a well-managed and organised operation and financial gain in offences falling into the 'exploitation' category would be aggravating, as would the age and vulnerability of the victim. The SAP advice regarding risk assessment and internet sex offenders is based upon a system developed by Taylor, Holland and Quayle (2001) on behalf of the COPINE (Combating of Paedophile Information Networks in Europe, University College, Cork) project. The typology developed by Taylor et al. (2001) lists ten categories of offence that increase in seriousness from level 1–9. Level 1 offences include images often freely available on the internet depicting children in their underwear or swimsuits, while levels 9 and 10 include grossly obscene and sadistic images of children. It is recognised that offenders may possess images that cross several categories, but that 'overt sexual intent and content' (2001, p 6) are key issues which the police and practitioners working with internet offenders presumably should address in assessing risk. Other factors which may impact upon risk assessment are identified as:

1   The size of a collection of images and the manner in which it is organised. This is taken to be indicative of the extent to which an offender is using such material offline.
2   New and private material is taken to be indicative of access to sex offender communities and possibly producers.
3   The child's age. It is argued that the younger the child the greater the imbalance of power between perpetrator and victim.

These levels of seriousness are based loosely on Quayle and Taylor's (2001) typology. Although this provides a valuable structure in which to locate different categories of internet sex offenders' use of indecent child images, there is no empirical evidence to suggest that the most serious level 4 and 5 internet offenders constitute the greatest risk to children in terms of contact offending. Findings from the author's recent research (Davidson, 2007) suggest that the system clouds the risk issue. An offender may, for example, possess images at level 1 but have regular access to children within his family circle, while another offender may possess images at level 3 but have no such contact and restrict his behaviour to the internet. Recent research undertaken by the author suggests that police practitioners who are working with internet sex offenders on a daily basis have identified very different types of behaviour among this group. It is apparent that some such offenders are not simply 'collectors' of images:

> I suspect that many internet sex offenders are really just sex offenders who now have access to the internet, with the advantages it affords in terms of access and anonymity and are not just 'collectors' at all. I recall a recent case, for example, involving an offender who claims the internet led him to offend. He had a senior job in the IT industry (very wealthy); he used the internet to target and groom a family with children. He started by using indecent images of young children but then arranged to meet the family and over a considerable period of time helped with

babysitting etc. and became trusted (typical grooming behaviour) – he eventually raped their young child. (R 7)

(Davidson, 2007)

While there is some limited research evidence to suggest that offenders collecting indecent images of children limit their offending behaviour to non-contact abuse (Quayle and Taylor (2002, 2003), a number of recent convictions under the Sexual Offences Act 2003 (England and Wales) suggest otherwise, and it seems unwise to make such assumptions on the basis of little empirical evidence. It is clear from some recently prosecuted cases that sex offenders are using the internet to contact other sex offenders, groom children for abuse and are collecting indecent internet images of children (Davidson and Martellozzo, 2008; Davidson, 2007). The maximum penalty for this new offence is ten years imprisonment. The definition of 'grooming' in the legislation is provided by the CPS (Figure 4.1).

<table>
<tr><td>

•   The offence only applies to adults.

•   There must be communication (a meeting or any other form of communication) on at least two previous occasions. It is not necessary for the communications to be of a sexual nature.

•   The communication can take place anywhere in the world.

•   The offender must either meet the child or travel to the pre-arranged meeting.

•   The meeting or at least part of the travel must take place within the jurisdiction.

•   The person must have an intention to commit any offence under Part I of the 2003 Act or any act done outside England and Wales, which would be an offence in the jurisdiction. This may be evident from the previous communications or other circumstances e.g., an offender travels in possession of ropes, condoms or lubricants etc.

•   The child is under 16 and the adult does not reasonably believe that the child is over 16. However, if this is not the case e.g., the child's place has been taken by an undercover police officer, an attempt could be charged.

</td></tr>
</table>

Figure 4.1 CPS definition of 'grooming'
Source: CPS (2007) *Sexual Offences Act 2003*

In sentencing under the 'sexual grooming'[2] (s 15) category, sentencers are advised to consider the following aggravating case circumstances:

- the seriousness of the intended offence (which will affect both the offender's culpability and the degree of risk to which the victim has been exposed);
- the degree to which the offence was planned;
- the sophistication of the grooming;
- the determination of the offender;
- how close the offender came to success;
- the reason why the offender did not succeed, that is, was it a change of mind or did someone or something prevent the offender from continuing;
- any physical or psychological injury suffered by the victim.

(Sentencing Guidelines Council, 2006, p 76)

Advice is provided to sentencers regarding the basis of sentencing decisions, which should be informed by pre-sentence reports produced by the Probation Service and psychiatric reports. Attendance at a community treatment programme can be a mandatory requirement of a community order. The explicit advice to sentencers regarding community orders for sex offenders is that:

a court should always consider a curfew requirement or a residence requirement, and should also consider passing other ancillary orders, for example a requirement to attend a special treatment programme designed to help an offender control and overcome any sexually deviant tendencies.

(SAP, 2006c, p 11)

SAP guidance refers to 'risk of re-offending' as a key concept in guiding risk assessment practice, following emphasis in the CJA 2003 upon protecting the public. To this end Part Two of the Sexual Offences Act 2003 introduced a number of new measures to place further restrictions on sex offenders' behaviour in the community:

---

2   Defined as 'An offender aged 18 or over meeting, or travelling to meet, a child under 16 (having met or communicated with the child on at least two previous occasions) with the intention of committing a sexual offence against the child', Sexual Offences Act 2003, s 15.

1   Notification order – requiring sex offenders convicted for sexual offences overseas to register in the UK.
2   Sexual offences prevention order (SOPO) – SOPOs can be made for those currently serving a community sentence, or for an offender who has a previous conviction for a sexual offence but whose behaviour indicates that they may re-offend.
3   Foreign travel order – may be used to prevent a person convicted of a sexual offence from travelling outside of the UK.
4   Risk of sexual harm order – may be used to protect a child where a person has engaged in sexually explicit conduct or communication with a child on at least two occasions.

Sentencing practice

A range of sentences are available under the Sexual Offences Act 2003, including a community rehabilitation order (formally a probation order), which may include a number of requirements (the SAP advice suggests that five is the maximum). Requirements include, for example, supervision with a probation officer; community work (unpaid); curfew; residence; programme attendance; and a range of treatments including those for mental health problems and alcohol abuse. The CJA 2003 introduced two sentencing provisions for sex offenders: indeterminate sentences of imprisonment for public protection (s 225(2), (3)) (persons aged 18 and over convicted of a 'serious' offence[3]) where the court considers that the offender poses a serious risk to the public; and extended sentences (s 227) enables the court to extend a sentence where a person aged 18 or more is convicted of an offence other than a serious offence (where the maximum sentence is between two and ten years) and the court considers that the offender poses a serious risk (SAP 2006d).

The use of custody for sex offenders as a group has fluctuated little over recent years, and rose by 5 per cent over a ten-year period between 1995 and 2005; 55 per cent were given immediate custodial sentences in 1995 compared to 60 per cent in 2005 (Home Office, 2007). The data produced below, provided by the Home Office, is not broken down by type of sexual offence or victim age – it is therefore impossible to explore sentencing disposal for those convicted of sexual offences involving children. The statistics

---

3   A serious offence is defined as where the maximum sentence is ten years or more (Criminal Justice Act 2003, s 224).

unfortunately reveal little about actual practice and the decisions underpinning case outcome; there is a scarcity of research in this area, but practice probably varies enormously. In recent research undertaken by the author (Davidson, 2007), for example, police practitioners expressed concern regarding variance in sentencing practice and particularly the way in which courts view the possession of indecent images of children. It was suggested that sentencers have different views regarding the seriousness of possession, on the basis that no *direct* victimisation appears to occur. Given that children are abused in the production of abusive images, it would appear that there is a need for clearer guidance from the SAP to sentencers regarding the possession of indecent images of children – one respondent commented:

> Another problem that we have in Scotland is variance in the judicial view regarding the possession of indecent images of children; it's a question of educating and raising awareness as some judges take a serious view of this form of offending and some don't, as they believe that there is no real victim.
>
> (R 10, Davidson, 2007)

This view was supported by the experience of a respondent working with sex offenders in Switzerland: The problem is that federal areas treat the offence differently in that some will remand these offenders into treatment and some will not. Some view this as an offence and some do not. There is no equity and sentencing varies by federal area.

(R 4, Davidson, 2007)

More research is needed into sentencing practice in this area.

Table 4.1 Sex offenders given immediate custody by sentence (sentenced at magistrates and Crown Court), England and Wales

Sentence	1995	1998	2001	2005
Young offender institution (YOI)	156	172	123	120
Immediate custody	2,418	2,687	2,400	2,701

Source: Home Office, 2007

Table 4.2 Average sentence length for sex and violent offenders sentenced for indictable offences, England and Wales

Offence group	Average sentence length (months)			
	1995	1998	1999	2005
Sexual offences	36.8	41.3	40.4	41.5
Violent against the person	22.2	22.1	22.6	24.5

Source: Home Office, 2007

The average prison sentence length for all sex offenders has increased from 36.8 months in 1995 to 41.5 months in 2005 (Table 4.2). The average sentence length for female sex offenders was 29.8 months in 2005, and the average for male sex offenders was 41.6 months in 2005 (Home Office, 2007).[4] Sex offenders continue to receive much longer prison sentences than offenders convicted for violent offences (24.5 months compared to 41.5 months in 2005 (Table 4.2)). It is clear that sex offenders are seen to pose a greater risk than other offenders – there is little government explanation for the disparity in sentence length between sex offenders and other 'dangerous' offenders. At a recent Prime Minister's Question Time the Prime Minister was asked if he thought sex offenders prison sentences should be shorter – the response was as follows:

> Government policy was to ensure that everything was done to encourage people to report sexual offences, rather than discourage them, and that was the criteria which we would apply. The PMOS (Prime Minister's Official Spokesman) also pointed out that we had introduced the ability to allow for offenders convicted of specific sexual offences, including rape, to remain in prison indefinitely until the level of risk to the public had been assessed as manageable. That did mean that in certain cases, if the level of risk could not be assessed as acceptable, people may never be released, so there was that fall-back. The PMOS said that primary basis by which we judged anything in

---

4   This data is out of date but is based upon the latest available information from the Home Office – Sentencing Statistics for England and Wales, 2005.

this area was to encourage people to report offences, rather than to discourage them.

(Downing Street Says Archives,
13 March 2006)

It is clearly the government's position that longer sentences reassure the public and encourage the reporting of abuse.

During 2005 4,700 sex offenders were sentenced, the majority of whom received a custodial sentence (2,700). A significant proportion (1,400 or 30 per cent) received a community sentence; however, only 593 received a community rehabilitation order (formerly a probation order).

More use was made of community sentences for sex offenders in 2005 (30 per cent) compared to data for 1995 (24 per cent), but considerably less use was made of the community rehabilitation order (formerly the probation order): only 8 per cent received the order in 2005 compared to 16.5 per cent in 1995 (Table 4.3). Sentencers made use of the new community order and referral orders in 2005 (Table 4.3), but these were employed in a minority of cases. It is of

Table 4.3 Sex offenders given community sentences by sentence, England and Wales, 1995 and 2005

	1995 thousands (%)	2005 thousands (%)
Total community sentence	1,139 (24)	1,444 (30)
Community rehabilitation order (formerly probation order)	763 (16.3)	593 (8)
Supervision order	184 (3.9)	177 (3.7)
Community punishment order (formerly community service)	127 (2.7)	84 (1.8)
Curfew order	–	44 (0.9)
Referral order (introduced 04/2002)	–	152 (3.2)
Community order (introduced 04/2005)	–	323 (6.8)

Source: Home Office, 2007

concern that some sentencers are still making use of the Community Punishment Order (CPO) (formally community service) as a sentencing option. The inappropriateness of this disposal as a sentencing option for sex offenders has been raised by commentators such as Beech et al. (1998), whose research demonstrates that a sentence involving a therapeutic component is preferable. The CPO is a community sentence whereby offenders undertake unpaid work in the community under the supervision of a probation officer. Such orders contain no treatment element and would not allow sex offenders to address their offending behaviour. CPOs are unsuitable for this group of offenders.

The statistics produced by the Home Office reflect the decision-making process regarding offenders within the criminal justice process. Bottomley and Pease (1986), while recognising the problems associated with the use of such data, have called for a re-evaluation of its worth in criminological research. The theoretical perspective adopted by Bottomley and Pease is concerned with the social construction of criminal statistics and the decision-making process. Several important stages in the process are identified, all of which affect directly the offences that are recorded: the first of these stages, and one which most directly affects statistics on sexual offending, is the recording of crimes reported to the police by witnesses and victims and those crimes discovered by the police.

Sex offender registration in the United Kingdom

The management of sex offenders in the community is supported by the present legislative framework (the Sex Offenders Act 1997; the Crime (Sentences) Act, 1997; and the sex offender orders introduced under the Crime and Disorder Act 1998 and later under the Sexual Offences Act 2003; the risk of sexual harm order introduced under the Sexual Offences Act 2003). All newly-convicted sex offenders are required to register under the Sex Offenders Act 1997 (strengthened by Part Two of the Sexual Offences Act 2003, which introduces a number of new orders), including those supervised in the community, those cautioned and those offenders released from prison. The duration of the registration requirement depends on sentence length, type of offence, age of the offender and age of the victim. The minimum period of registration is five years and the maximum an 'indefinite period' for sentences of 30 months or

Sentence	Notification period
Life imprisonment or for a term of 30 months or more	An indefinite period
Those admitted to a hospital subject to a restriction order	An indefinite period
Imprisonment for a term of more than 6 months but less than 30 months	10 years
Imprisonment for a term of 6 months or less	7 years
Those admitted to a hospital without being subject to a restriction order	7 years
Other sentences	5 years
Those cautioned 80(1)(d)	2 years

Figure 4.2 Sentence and notification period for sexual offenders
Source: Adapted from the Sexual Offences Act 2003, s 82

more in custody. These arrangements follow automatically on conviction and are not as such a part of the sentencing process, but sentencers have a duty to inform offenders about the requirement at the point of sentence. Sentencers may consider extended periods on licence for sex offenders where risk to the public is considered high (CJA 2003, ss 225–229). The period of registration or notification varies by sentence length under the Sexual Offences Act 2003 (s 82) (Figure 4.2).

There are currently plans to introduce some public notification regarding the whereabouts of those on the sex offenders register, and full notification may be introduced to UK legislation following the United States example.

Registration and public notification in the United States

The Jacob Wetterling Crimes Against Children and Sexually Violent Offender Act (1994) was introduced following the abduction and disappearance of 11-year-old Jacob Wetterling in 1989. The legislation requires sex offender registration with local law enforcement agencies. Megan's Law (1996), following the abduction and murder of Megan Kanka, amends the Wetterling Act, requiring states to establish a community notification system. This legislation introduced the concept of public notification when sex offenders move into a community. The Pam Lychner Sexual Offender and Tracking Act 1996 formed an amendment to the Wetterling Act requiring life registration for repeat offenders and other serious sex offenders (US Department of Justice, 2007).

States have different approaches to disclosure – many categorise offenders into three risk bands. Level 1 offenders may remain known only to law enforcement agencies, and information regarding level 2 offenders would be distributed to organisations such as schools, but would not be made public. Level 3 offenders are considered high risk and in New Jersey, for example, full disclosure to the community is common: the form the disclosure takes varies across states (Figure 4.3). Police officers in Washington organise community notification meetings to inform communities about offenders (Hebenton and Thomas, 1997). Recent research exploring the effectiveness of different notification procedures suggests that when a more aggressive approach to notification is used, such as house leafleting or community notification meetings, the community

---

- Community leaflet drop – the distribution of leaflets to households containing details about the location of sex offenders recently moving to the area, with photographs.

- County sheriffs' websites – web pages containing information about sex offenders in the community and their risk level, including photographs. Or information can be sent to individuals on provision of their address when a sex offender moves within a certain radius of their home. See Fairfield (Ohio) County Sheriffs Office website for an example of this approach at www.sheriff.fairfield.oh.us/sexoffenders.html.

- Community notification meetings – police officers inform communities via meetings often advertised by press release. For an example, see City of Eagan press release at www.ci.eagan.mn.us/live/news.asp?menu=2207&id=12574.

- Information about sex offenders residing in a community displayed in a public area, such as a library.

Figure 4.3 Forms of sex offender community disclosure in the United States

is more informed about sex offenders than when a more passive approach is used (library notices, for example). However, the nature of the notification strategy does not appear to have an impact upon the communities' perception of the degree of risk or preventative action taken (Beck and Travis, 2006).

The effectiveness of registration and notification is questionable. Such legislation assumes that the majority of sexual abuse is perpetrated by strangers; however, research indicates that children are much more likely to be abused by someone they know, often a family member (Winick, 1998). Prentky (1996) suggests that notification laws may simply displace sex offender behaviour, as offenders may simply commit crimes in different areas, away from the scrutiny of their neighbours. He also points out that there are no guarantees regarding the public response to notification. Some researchers have asked sex offenders for their views about the effectiveness of registration and notification. In Levenson and Cotter's (2005) study of 183 sex offenders recently released for custody in Florida, approximately 30 per cent reported harassment, the loss of employment or damage to their property. Approximately 20 per cent believed that registration would make communities safer. These findings are supported by research conducted in Kentucky by Tewksbury (2005) with a sample of 121 sex offenders. This research concludes that public notification results in the isolation and harassment of sex offenders, who have difficulty in finding employment and in rebuilding their lives. Tewksbury also makes the important point that notification can be equally stigmatising for an offender's family if they are known in a community.

Trial by media: newspaper response to UK government sentencing policy

Newspaper coverage of sentencing practice for sex offenders, particularly child sexual abusers, is frequent: the treatment and behaviour of sex offenders is brought to the public's attention on a regular basis. This coverage has been and continues to be highly critical of the government and the judiciary. Common story themes in both the tabloids and the broadsheets are: dangerous offenders are given prison sentences that are too short; the government appears to be powerless in controlling the behaviour of the judiciary in sentencing sex offenders; the incompetence of the Home Office and successive Home Secretaries; the recent overcrowding crisis in prisons has led to sex offenders receiving community and suspended sentences rather than prison sentences. In June 2006 the *Daily Mail* ran the following headline: 'Blair in a Panic over Sentencing' (15 June 2006), claiming that the government were involved in a 'scramble' to introduce more legislation following the early release of 53 dangerous offenders sentenced to life over the last six years. The previous day the *Mail* had led with: 'Outrage over Five Week Sentence for Paedophile' (14 June 2006), with a clear photograph of the offender, suggesting that increasingly short prison sentences are being given to child sexual abusers and citing the example of Richard Bruce, who had received a prison sentence of 27 months, but who would probably be released after 13 months having been remanded in custody for a year prior to trial. The newspaper took the opportunity to criticise the Home Secretary and government policy: 'The case piled further pressure on Home Secretary John Reid to overhaul sentencing guidelines, after serial paedophile Craig Sweeney was given a tariff of just five years on Monday for kidnapping and attacking a three-year-old girl.'

In August the *Mail* voiced concern over a sentencer's decision to use a community sentence (supervision order) for a young offender who sexually abused a girl (*Daily Mail*, 4 August 2006). The judge justified the decision on the basis that the knife was only used to prevent the victim from disclosing the abuse and that the victim was not abused at 'knifepoint'.

In September 2006 the *Mirror*, commenting on a child abuser who had re-offended, headlined:

> Free to Rape Paedo on the Run Hours after Release from Jail – Fugitive pervert Paul Redpath only got out of jail this week, it emerged last night. The sick sex offender was released after serving 18 months for an indecent assault on a 13-year-old girl.
> (30 September 2006)

Redpath was given a three-year custodial sentence and a three-year probation term, but was in fact released into a probation hostel early because he had served more than a year on remand in custody. He breached probation conditions by failing to return to his secure accommodation (BBC News, 26 October 2006).

In October 2006 the *Mirror* declared 'Justice is Just a Joke', commenting 'It's condemnation indeed that we're not surprised to hear of the judge who freed an alleged rapist on bail' (24 October 2006).

The broadsheet newspapers have added their voice in criticism of the government and the sentencing of sex offenders, most notably following sex offender Craig Sweeney's case and Home Secretary John Reid's claim that the sentence was too lenient. Sentencing Craig Sweeney to life imprisonment at Cardiff Crown Court for the abduction and sexual assault of a child, Judge John Griffith Williams QC stated that he should not be considered for parole for at least five years, and that this would be dependent upon his risk assessment. When John Reid objected to the sentence along with the victim's family in October 2006, *The Times* mocked 'Get Some Policies, Mr Reid, and Stop Hiding Behind an Odious Sex Offender':

> Talk about a soft target: of all the parade of grotesques who pass through the courts, Craig Sweeney is especially horrifying. To abduct and sexually assault a three-year-old girl, twice, before terrifying her with a 100 mph chase with a police car and then throwing her out of a vehicle on to the side of the road to be found by the police later does, as the judge in the case commented, beggar belief. For a Home Secretary looking for tough headlines, this must have appeared an easy one: Sweeney's sentence was too lenient and the case should be reconsidered, demanded John Reid publicly. In speaking out so quickly, our new Home Secretary engaged his mouth before his brain, and not for the first time. Never mind for a moment that his intervention may make an appeal against the sentence harder to win, which is the objection made known by Lord Goldsmith, the Attorney General. Look instead at the fact that Mr Reid is railing against government policy. It is the Government that decided to formalise the introduction of an automatic discount for a guilty plea, which is what has made Sweeney's sentence sound so potentially low.
>
> (*The Times*, 13 June 2006)

In January 2007 the public were made aware of the deepening overcrowding crisis in British prisons and the impact of this upon the sentencing of some sex offenders. Blaming the government, the *Mail* suggested that an internet sex offender, Derek Williams, received a suspended sentence as the judge was aware of a Home Office request to send few offenders to prison: (*Daily Mail*, 26 January 2007). Other newspapers agreed: 'Release of Paedophiles Embarrasses Government' proclaimed the *Mirror*, suggesting a rift between the Prime Minster Tony Blair and the Home Secretary John Reid regarding the sentencing of 'dangerous offenders':

> Prime Minister Tony Blair scrambled to avert a political crisis on Friday after judges freed two convicted paedophiles in response to a government warning about full prisons. Home Secretary John Reid had written to judges asking them to send criminals to jail only if necessary because of a lack of cells. The release of two paedophiles prompted Blair to deny Reid had ordered the courts to free dangerous criminals.
>
> (25 January 2007)

The situation appeared to worsen for the Labour Government in January 2007 when the *Mirror* described recent sentencing of child sexual abusers as 'Indecent', commenting that:

> Paedophiles who prey on young girls are serving less than two years in jail, it was revealed yesterday. Average sentences for indecent assault and other lewd offences are as low as 17 months. The Nexus Institute, which works with victims, claimed their clients had been let down by the justice system.
>
> (26 January 2007)

Indeterminate sentencing and civil commitment of sex offenders: future trends?

Some countries have passed legislation that allows for the detention and supervision of sex offenders beyond sentence completion. In the UK the Crime and Disorder Act 1998 allowed courts to extend periods of supervision beyond custodial sentences where a person was considered to be at risk of further offending. The Sexual Offences Act 2003 now allows sentencers to pass determinate sentences on completion of a custodial sentence for sexual and violent offenders considered to be high risk. The CPS provides the following advice:

> These (determinate) sentences will be imposed when an adult offender who is convicted of a specified offence, and who the court considers is dangerous, *must* be sentenced to an extended sentence. An offender is dangerous if 'the court is of the opinion

that there is a significant risk to members of the public of serious harm occasioned by the commission by him of further specified offences.

(CPS, 2006)

The Sexual Offences Act 2003 also allows sentencers to pass indeterminate custodial sentences for public protection (at the point of sentence) for very high risk offenders. In such cases release is not automatic and must be approved by a parole board. The court sets a minimum term before which a case can be considered for parole. Following release the offender will remain on licence for a period of ten years.

In a similar fashion in Australia, the High Court, in *Attorney General vs Fardon* ((2004) 210 ALR 50), upheld the Queensland Dangerous Prisoners (Sexual Offences) Act (2003), which allows for the detention of sex offenders beyond sentence where offenders are considered to be at high risk of re-offending. Fardon was originally sentenced to 13 years imprisonment for rape in 1980. He was released on parole after eight years. Three weeks after his release he committed another rape and was sentenced to 14 years in custody. An application was made to detain Fardon indefinitely under section 13 of the 2003 Act. Following a four-day hearing an indefinite order was made. Fardon was granted leave to appeal by the High Court but the appeal was rejected (High Court of Australia, 2004). The Australian Government then introduced the Serious Sex Offenders Monitoring Act in 2005, which allows an order to be made on sentence completion for up to a further 15 years of supervision and/or treatment (Sullivan et al., 2005).

In the United States sentencers also have the power to detain sex offenders indefinitely; the system differs from the UK in that the decision to detain indefinitely is made at the end of the period of imprisonment and no minimum term for parole review is set, as the detention takes the form of a civil commitment on mental health grounds. This could lead to incarceration with no opportunity to appeal for life. A US Supreme Court ruling (by a 5:4 majority) in June 1997 held that sex offenders could be subject to indefinite civil commitment in a psychiatric institution if, due to a 'personality disorder' or 'mental abnormality', they are deemed to be at a high risk of perpetrating further sexual offences. This ruling followed the case of Leroy Hendricks, a convicted sex offender who had served a prison sentence but whom the state of Kansas still wished to detain.

In *Kansas v Hendricks* (Case no 95-1694) the Supreme Court upheld a Kansas law (the Sexually Violent Predator Act (1994)) that permits civil commitment on completion of a custodial sentence. The ruling has been criticised heavily by psychiatrists. The President of the American Psychiatric Association, Herbert Sacks, has commented on the inappropriateness of using psychiatric care in the social control of sex offenders, and refers to the possibility that psychiatric hospitals may become alternative prisons. Others have raised concerns about the definition of mental illness employed in considering civil commitment: Alexander (2000) suggests that offenders should have a serious mental illness and constitute a danger to others before civil commitment is considered. He claims that minor mental health disorders, such as paraphilia disorder and anti-social personality, are being used unfairly to justify indefinite commitment.

The use of civil commitment for sex offenders has spread to 19 other US states, despite protests made by the psychiatric profession, civil rights campaigners and some sections of the legal profession. In 2007 the New York Court of Appeals ruled that a court could not simply invoke a civil commitment order for a sex offender without first holding a hearing to establish how far the offender met the specified mental health criteria (Bryant, 2007). The National Association of Criminal Defense Lawyers (NACDL) in the United States has recently voiced concern about the use of civil commitment orders on legal grounds, claiming that the full range of due process rights should apply before the imposition of such orders, including the right to trial by jury and the right to present evidence (NACDL, 2007). The NACDL believes that civil commitment orders constitute a threat to civil liberties: 'Because the liberty interest implicated by a civil commitment statutes is similar to that effected in criminal trials, the person facing civil commitment should be afforded all of the same rights afforded to a criminal defendant' (2007, p 9).

Aldhous (2007), writing in the *New Scientist*, claims that 3,646 sex offenders, who had completed their prison sentences, were being held in US mental institutions under the civil commitment ruling in May 2006. Despite the considerable civil liberties implication of detention beyond sentence on civil commitment orders, serious questions have been raised by the psychiatric profession about the ability of mental health services to indefinitely 'police' this expanding group. Wakefield (2006) suggests that the orders constitute an exercise in costly preventative detention, with little treatment offered or prospect of release. Lieb (2006) estimates that the total annual cost of maintaining current civil commitment orders in the United States is $224,000,000. Janus (2004) describes the media coverage and consequent public outrage in Wisconsin when 30 sex offenders subject to civil commitment orders were released early. Although none of the offenders were convicted for further sexual offences, the criteria for civil commitment changed within the legislation from 'substantially probable' to re-offend to 'probable' to re-offend. Consequently release is now infrequent. An article in the *New York Times* (4 March 2007) claimed that civil commitment orders fail in their aim to treat and rehabilitate offenders, as only a small proportion of offenders complete treatment programmes and are considered eligible for release. The example of 72-year-old Leroy Hendricks is cited. A convicted child abuser from Kansas who completed his prison sentence 13 years ago, Hendricks is an invalid who spends most of his time in a wheelchair – he has failed to 'graduate' from treatment and has made unsuccessful appeals to the Supreme Court. He now accepts that he will probably not live to see his release. The paper also claims that some of the committed offenders are not among the most violent or the most serious. A case in Wisconsin involving a committed exhibitionist (indecent exposure) aged 102 is cited by way of example.

The *New York Times* (op. cit.) claims that 250 offenders have been released unconditionally in the United States since the introduction of the civil commitment legislation in 1990, approximately 50 per cent of whom were released on a legal technicality and not because they were deemed 'safe'. The article further claims that the extension of such schemes is popular with politicians seeking votes and striving to keep as many sex offenders locked up as possible, and that legislation agreed by President Bush at federal level pledges cash incentives to states detaining sex offenders beyond custody.

The expanding use of civil commitment for sex offenders in the United States would seem to be an attempt to impose long-term detention upon a problematic group of offenders outside of the criminal justice system, effectively passing the sex offender management problem to mental health services. This results in a 'win–win' situation for criminal justice agencies seeking to remove sex offenders from the community and for the government seeking to persuade an angry public of its ability to 'deal' effectively with the problem.

Key chapter themes

- The Labour Government has introduced a range of measures designed to manage and control sex offenders in the community, introduced in large part via the Sexual Offences Act 2003 and the Criminal Justice Act 2003.

- Broadsheet and tabloid newspaper reporting of sentencing practice has been frequent and highly critical of both government policy and the Home Secretary. This has led to the introduction of measures increasingly designed to monitor and control sex offenders in the community.

- Sentencers are now able to pass indeterminate sentences for sex offenders in the United Kingdom and Australia. The large number of sex offenders detained indefinitely under civil commitment legislation beyond custodial sentences on mental health grounds in the United States gives cause for concern and has been heavily criticised by the psychiatric and legal professions.

References

Aldhous, P, 'Sex offenders: Throwing away the key', *New Scientist*, 21 February 2007, accessed June 2007, www.newscientist.com/channel/opinion/mg19325924.200-sex-offenders-throwing-away-the-key.html

Alexander, R, 'Civil commitment of sex offenders to mental institutions should the standard be based on serious mental illness or mental disorder?', *Journal of Health and Social Policy*, 11(3) (2000), pp 67–78

Ashworth, A, *Principles of Criminal Law* (3rd edn), 1999, New York: Oxford University Press

Beck, V S and Travis, L 'Sex offender notification: A cross state comparison', *Police Practice and Research*, 7(4) (2006), pp 293–307

Beech, A, Fisher, D, Beckett, R and Fordham, A S, 'STEP 3: An evaluation of the prison sex offender treatment programme', 1998, Home Office Research, Development and Statistics Occasional Paper, London: Home Office

Bottomley, K and Pease, K, *Crime and Punishment*, 1986, London: Routledge

Bryant, B, 'Sex-offender commitments hit legal roadblock in NY', *Psychiatry News*, 42(3) (February 2007), p 17, accessed May 2007, www.pn. psychiatryonline.org/cgi/content/full/42/3/17

Crown Prosecution Service, *Sexual Offences Act 2003*, 2007, accessed May 2007, www.cps.gov.uk/legal/section7/chapter_a.html#

Davidson, J, 'Current practice and research into internet sex offending', 2007, Report prepared on behalf of the Risk Management Authority (Scotland)

Davidson, J and Martellozzo, E, 'Protecting children in cyberspace', in Letherby, G, Birch, P, Cain, M and Williams, K (eds), *Sex Crime* (forthcoming, March 2008), London: Willan Publishing

Downing Street Says Archives, Prime Minister's speech, 13 March 2006, www.downingstreetsays.org/archives/002471.html

Grinfeld, M J, 'Sexual predator ruling raises ethical, moral dilemma: Supreme Court OKs indefinite commitment for sex offenders', *Psychiatric Times*, XIV(8) (August 1997), p 1, accessed November 2006, www. psychiatrictimes.com/p970801b.html

Hebenton, B and Thomas, T, 'Keeping track: Observations on sex offenders registers in the US', *Home Office Crime Detection and Prevention Series*, Paper 83, Webb, B (ed), 1997, Police Research Group, London: HMSO

High Court of Australia, *Robert John Fardon v Rodney Jon Welford, Attorney General for the State of Queensland*, 1 October 2004, Public Information Office, accessed May 2007, www.hcourt.gov.au

Home Office, 'Regulatory impact assessment: Making provision in the management of offenders and sentencing bill for the mandatory polygraph testing of certain sexual offenders', 2006, London: HMSO

Home Office, 'Sentencing statistics 2005, England & Wales', RDS NOMS, 2007, Statistical bulletin

Janus, E S, 'Closing Pandora's box: Sexual predators and the politics of sexual violence', *Seton Hall Law Review*, 34(4) (2004), pp 1233–53

Levenson, J S and Cotter, L P, 'The effect of Megan's Law on sex offender re-integration', *Journal of Contemporary Criminal Justice*, 21 (2005), pp 49–66

Lieb, R, 'Comparison of state laws on involuntary commitment of sexually violent predators', *Sex Offender Law Report*, 7(2) (2006), 17, pp 26–32

National Association of Criminal Defense Lawyers, 'Report of the sex offender policy task force', 24 February 2007, www.nacdl.org/sl_docs. nsf/issues/sexoffender_attachments/$FILE/SexOffenderPolicy

New York Times, 'Doubts rise as States hold sex offenders after prison', 4 March 2007, www.nytimes.com/2007/03/04/us/04civil.html?ex=133066 4400&en=4b5d93af1ae8077f&ei=5088&partner

Prentky, R A, 'Community notification and constructive risk reduction', *Journal of Interpersonal Violence*, 11(2) (1996), pp 295–98

Quayle, E and Taylor, M, 'Child seduction and self-representation on the internet', *Cyberpsychology and Behaviour*, 4(5) (2001), pp 597–607

Quayle, E and Taylor, M, 'Paedophiles, pornography and the internet: Assessment issues', *British Journal of Social Work*, 32 (2002), pp 863–75

Quayle, E and Taylor, M, 'Model of problematic Internet use in people with a sexual interest in children', *Cyberpsychology and Behaviour*, 6(1) (2003), pp 93–106

Sentencing Advisory Panel, 'Sexual Offences Act 2003: The panels advice to the sentencing guidelines council', 2006a, www.sentencing-guidelines. gov.uk/docs/advice-sexual-offences.pdf

Sentencing Advisory Panel, 'Sexual Offences Act 2003: Consultation guideline', 2006b, www.sentencing-guidelines.gov.uk/docs/draft-guidelines-sexual-offences.pdf

Sentencing Advisory Panel, 'Sentencing guidelines on sexual offences consultation paper', 2006c, www.sentencing-guidelines.gov.uk/docs/draft-guidelines-sexual-offences.pdf

Sentencing Advisory Panel, 'Press release: Consultation guidelines on Sexual Offences Act 2003 (7 June 2006)', 2006d, www.sentencing-guidelines. gov.uk/docs/SOA2003-Definitive-press.pdf

Sullivan, D H, Mullen, P E and Pathe, M, 'Legislation in Victoria on sexual offenders: Issues for health professionals', *Medical Journal of Australia*, 183(6) (2005), pp 318–21

Taylor, M, Holland, G and Quayle, E, 'Typology of paedophile picture collections', *The Police Journal*, 74 (2001), pp 97–107

Tewksbury, R, 'Collateral consequences of sex offender registration', *Journal of Contemporary Criminal Justice*, 21(1) (2005), pp 67–81

United States Department of Justice, *Overview and history of the Jacob Wetterling Act*, 2007, accessed July 2007, www.ojp.usdoj.gov/BJA/what/2a1jwacthistory.html

Wakefield, H, 'The vilification of sex offenders: Do laws targeting sex offenders increase recidivism and sexual violence?', paper presented at the 22nd Annual Symposium of the American College of Forensic Psychology, 17 March 2006, San Francisco, California

Winick, B J, 'Sex offender law in the 1990s: A therapeutic jurisprudence analysis', *Psychology, Public Policy, and Law*, 4(1/2) (1998), pp 505–70

Chapter 5

The management, control and treatment of child sexual abusers

This chapter seeks to:

- Explore government approaches to the risk assessment, management and control of child sexual abusers.

- Explore government approaches to the treatment of child sexual abusers, including those abusers using the internet to access children.

- Consider media response to the management of sex offenders in the community.

Assessing and managing child sexual abusers: a 'risky' business

A growing awareness of the scale and the consequences of child abuse filtered into the criminal justice system during the 1980s, accompanied by a recognition on the part of criminal justice agencies charged with the 'management' and 'supervision' of serious offenders that public confidence largely rested upon a perceived ability to prevent re-offending. In the past it had been sufficient to send large numbers of child abusers to prison but media reports about early release, community placement in hostels and re-offending did not cast those charged with responsibility for such offenders in a good light. The 1980s and 1990s saw the large-scale development of community probation treatment programmes for sex offenders and the development of the prison Sex Offender Treatment Programme (SOTP), and more recently the internet Sex Offender Treatment Programme (i-SOTP) in 2006. The message seemed to be clear: the incidence of child sexual abuse was higher than had been estimated – a 'tougher' more treatment-based approach was needed to deal with such high risk sex offenders, and a developing groundswell in public anxiety regarding the incidence and nature of child abuse and criminal justice response to the perpetrators needed to be addressed.

Newspaper reporting and the management of child sexual abusers

While newspaper reporting of the role of social welfare agencies involved in key child protection cases such as Cleveland and Climbie was highly critical, the apparent inability of criminal justice practitioners to recognise and act upon the 'risk' posed to the public by sex offenders and other serious offenders continues to be a source of constant media criticism. The *Daily Mirror* has been particularly critical of decisions made by criminal justice agencies concerning sex offenders, employing headlines intended to fuel public anxiety: 'Murderer Let Out of Prison to Rape: Victim was Boy Aged 10' (27 April 2006). The front page article claimed that: 'A murderer who raped a boy of 10 just months after release from a life sentence was yesterday told he must die in jail.' The newspaper picked up the story of Anthony Rice, a sex offender who was released from prison and then committed murder: 'Blunders Let Serial Sex Attacker Out to Kill.' Blaming 'blundering officials' who were responsible for his release, it claimed: 'a string of failures by probation officers and the parole board allowed him out and nine months later he brutally murdered' (*Daily Mirror*, 11 May 2006).

On this theme, the *Daily Express* alerted the public to under-resourcing in the Probation Service and the possible consequences with the headline 'Perils Posed by Overloaded Probation Service':

> The public cannot be fully protected from dangerous offenders because probation officers are overloaded, a watchdog warned yesterday. Chief Inspector of Probation Andrew Bridges said most frontline officers handle more than 30 cases each and would do a 'better job' if they had fewer. It came as police chief Terry Grange said he could not promise the public 'absolute safety' or that dangerous offenders will not offend again. The messages

follow a series of high-profile killings by offenders under supervision and are a further blow to John Reid as he tries to get a grip
on the Home Office.

(12 February 2007, copyright
Express Newspapers)

Other stories have focused upon the role of 'blundering officials'
in similar cases. Another headline exclaimed: 'Girl of 9 Raped by
"Supervised" Paedo – Registered Sex Offender Abused Child for
Three Years', the article went on to say that 'A known paedophile
who repeatedly raped a nine-year-old girl despite being under
community supervision was jailed indefinitely yesterday' (*Daily
Mirror*, 21 April 2006). This story criticises the National Probation
Service for its failure to properly supervise and manage a supervised
sex offender in the community. In another article the paper suggests
that the Prison Service is equally inept at controlling the behaviour
of such offenders in custody: 'Pervert Runs Child Abuse Website
From His Jail Cell – Shamed Tutor is Paedophile "Agony Uncle": A
twisted teacher jailed for downloading 11,000 vile images of children
is masterminding a website for paedophiles from behind bars' (*Daily
Mirror*, 31 August 2005).

Broadsheet and tabloid newspapers have criticised the Labour
Government's inability to control and monitor sex offenders, and
have been particularly critical of the Home Office following the
recent admission that approximately 300 registered sex offenders
had provided inaccurate registered addresses and had effectively
disappeared. *The Times* headlined: 'Sex Offenders Give Police the
Slip with Inaccurate Addresses' and commented that:

> Last night there was further embarrassment for the Home
> Office when a police leader said that the department had been
> given a warning about the problem three years ago. Jan Berry,
> chairwoman of the Police Federation, which represents rank-
> and-file officers, said that the organisation had alerted the
> Home Office to the issue but it had failed to come up with a
> solution.
>
> (29 January 2007)

The *Sun* headlined '322 Sex Fiends on the Loose' (27 January 2007),
blaming 'bungling police' for the missing offenders and also blaming
the inadequacy of Multi-Agency Public Protection Arrangements

(MAPPA). The *Daily Express* led with a scathing attack on the Home Office:

> Rapists and Child Sex Offenders Go Free: Thousands of rapists and paedophiles are still on the streets under Britain's soft justice. The scandal-hit Home Office now faces further fury over 7,200 sex offenders who were given only a caution for their crimes in just five years. A growing number of evil perverts are escaping court trials as prison chiefs battle with over crowded jails.
>
> (5 February 2007, copyright
> *Express Newspapers*)

It could be argued that such headlines are coming to reflect a growing public dissatisfaction with criminal justice response to 'dangerous' offenders; a dissatisfaction that the government are aware of and one that is increasingly reflected in moves to manage and control serious offenders. Home Secretary John Reid's speech to the Parole Board in 2006 reflects this anxiety:

> Keeping the public safe is the first duty of government. A government, which fails in that, has no right to be a government. The public has the right to expect that everything possible will be done to minimise the risk from serious violent or dangerous offenders and the right to feel that this is happening and that sufficient priority is being given to that. What is our current problem? It is quite simple: The public feel that the system in so many occasions is just not working on their behalf and they are losing confidence, fast and we need to restore it fast.
>
> (Home Secretary's Annual Speech to the
> Parole Board, May 2006)

Other newspapers have focused upon the inadequacies of the sex offender register in enabling monitoring of dangerous sex offenders: 'Sex Offender Who Murdered Schoolgirl Went Unchecked After Name Change' – claiming that a sex offender who abused and murdered a child on release from prison was able to avoid the police by providing a false name (*Daily Mail*, 8 November 2006). The *Daily Mail* has increasingly used such stories to criticise the Labour Government and the Home Office: 'Police Have "Lost Track" of More Than 300 Sex Offenders' (*Daily Mail*, 29 January 2007). The paper also claimed that the police had informed the Home Office that several hundred sex offenders were untraceable several years ago (*Daily Mail*, 28 January 2007).

Government control, management and treatment of child sexual abusers

The Labour Government, through its criminal justice agencies, has sought to control and manage child sexual abusers in a number of ways: the National Probation Service, along with the police, play a central role in the provision of external controls on sex offenders in the community, through statutory supervision in the form of community rehabilitation orders or through supervision following release from prison. Key factors in exercising this control are considered to be:

- effective risk assessment and management
- the motivation not to offend
- effective treatment programmes
- supportive environment
- regular supervision
- external monitoring
- restrictions on movements and associations
- curfews
- sex offender orders
- electronic tagging
- surveillance
- effective Multi-Agency Public Protection Arrangements (MAPPA).

(Home Office, 2002)

The National Probation Service in England and Wales (Criminal Justice Social Work in Scotland) has taken increasing responsibility over the past 20 years for the supervision of some serious offenders in the community. Sentencers are more likely to impose a custodial sentence upon offenders convicted of child sexual abuse related offences in the wake of media attention and public anxiety regarding this group. However, the National Probation Service will inevitably have some significant input to their sentence: sex offenders considered 'low risk' may be subject to a community sentence and undertake the Home Office accredited SOTP or the recently introduced i-SOTP, and incarcerated offenders will be subject to a period of post-release probation supervision. The Prison Service has provided a treatment programme for sex offenders since the early 1990s, which is largely based upon the probation model, SOTP.

In the UK all sex offenders are subject to the restrictions placed upon them by MAPPA.[1] These arrangements require criminal justice, housing, health, local authority, social work and probation services to put into place arrangements for establishing and monitoring risk with sex offenders and violent offenders. The Criminal Justice and Court Services Act (2000) formalised MAPPA arrangements by placing a statutory duty on police and probation, working jointly as the responsible authority in each area, to establish arrangements for the assessment and management of the risk posed by such offenders. The CJA 2003 (ss 325–327) extends the definition of 'responsible authority' to include the Prison Service; establishes a reciprocal 'duty to co-operate' between the responsible authority and a range of other authorities and social care agencies; and requires the Secretary of State to appoint two lay advisers to assist with the strategic review of arrangements in each area. In Scotland MAPPA arrangements have recently been introduced (September 2006), and legislation amending the Sexual Offences Act 2003 has recently come into force (Police, Public Order and Criminal Justice (Scotland) Act 2006).[2]

MAPPA arrangements address several areas of good practice: ongoing risk assessment; the development of risk management plans that focus upon public protection; and service performance evaluation. There are several core functions: identifying MAPPA offenders; sharing relevant information across agencies involved in the assessment of risk; and assessing and managing risk of serious harm. A responsibility is placed upon the Prison Service,

1 Established by the Criminal Justice and Court Services Act 2000 and re-enacted and strengthened by the CJA 2003 in England and Wales and by the Management of Offenders (Scotland) Act 2005 in Scotland.

2 Section 80 of the Police, Public Order and Criminal Justice (Scotland) Act 2006 amends the Sexual Offences Act 2003 by inserting s 96A. Police can apply to a sheriff to obtain a warrant to enter and search a known (registered) sex offender's home address for risk assessment purposes or following failure to gain entry on more that one occasion.

the police and local authorities to jointly establish arrangements for the risk assessment and management of sex offenders subject to the notification requirements of Part 2 of the Sexual Offences Act 2003.

In England, Scotland and Wales violent and sex offenders are divided into three distinct categories under MAPPA arrangements: Category One includes all registered sex offenders; Category Two includes violent offenders; and Category Three includes offenders with previous convictions whose behaviour suggests that they pose a continuing risk. Level 1 offenders (considered to be the least serious group) are overseen by one agency, usually the police or National Probation Service, while level 2 offenders are subject to multi-agency oversight and level 3 offenders (known as the critical few and considered to pose the most risk) may be subject to intensive measures, such as monitoring on a daily basis by a private care firm or police surveillance.

Recent research conducted by the author has explored the views of criminal justice practitioners about the effectiveness of MAPPA arrangements (Davidson, 2007). The system appears to be fairly unique, particularly in Europe where communication between agencies is more informal. However, while respondents supported the principle of multi-agency working and MAPPA arrangements, some questioned the adequacy of the system in assessing and managing risk with sex offenders and claimed that under-resourcing continues to be a key issue. One police respondent noted:

> MAPPA was introduced in 1998 (England and Wales). It's good for re-housing sex offenders but fairly ineffective truthfully in managing and monitoring this group. When you think about the scale of the problem, 4,000 new sex offenders are registered every year; how can you realistically monitor that number of people? It's a resource issue and there is no real mechanism for knowing if someone is high risk and following up on that information; it may be a better idea to monitor the most serious more closely. (R 3)

A sentiment echoed by another senior police officer: 'It [MAPPA] is certainly a step in the right direction, but is this really a priority for the agencies involved? It's not really, and resourcing is an issue' (R 5). The respondent went on to suggest that MAPPA officers should be more pro-active in 'dip-sampling' from the sex offenders register on a regular basis and making unannounced visits to view sex offenders' homes and their computers:

> MAPPA Officers should be regularly 'dip-sampling' from the register to check all sex offenders and should be checking out their lifestyles regularly. They should be checking internet sex offenders' computers on a regular basis – in fact they should be checking all sex offenders' computers. Resourcing is however a big issue here. (R 5)

Controlling child sexual abusers: restricting behaviour and lie detection

Information regarding all cautioned and convicted sex offenders is now stored on a central database developed by the police and the Probation Service. ViSOR, the Violent Sex Offender Register, was introduced in 2004 and contains information on sexual and violent offenders, including basic demographic details and agency reports. Limited use of electronic tagging, first introduced in the Criminal Justice Act 1991, has been made in an attempt to restrict the movements of sex offenders. Use is limited, as sex offenders are excluded from the home detention curfew arrangements. A small number of sex offenders have been tagged voluntarily. Tagging involves offenders wearing a battery-operated tag and receiver unit; the location of the unit can be tracked by satellite or mobile phone masts. Information regarding location would then be transmitted to a control centre. The information could be relayed in real time or downloaded at the end of each day when the unit was placed in a docking device. The Home Office and the National Probation Service will probably introduce polygraph testing (lie detection) in managing and monitoring sex offenders in the community. The testing will be used alongside the accredited treatment programme. Offenders will take a test every six months to explore response to treatment and risk; it is argued that this will result in more accurate risk prediction and treatment evaluation.

The Home Office may introduce software to monitor computer use among sex offenders convicted of internet-related offences – recent research suggests that police practitioners do not consider that enough is presently being done to monitor this group of offenders under MAPPA arrangements. It was suggested that police officers should have unlimited access to registered sex offenders' home computers and that MAPPA officers should regularly make unannounced visits to sex offenders in order to view home environments and computers (Davidson, 2007).

The effectiveness of such measures in monitoring and managing child sexual abusers is questionable. There is very limited use of electronic tagging, and without the necessary resources to follow up suspected transgressions the use of tagging appears pointless and the extent to which this technology might really prevent offenders from frequenting public areas in which children are present is highly questionable. In recent research Grubin (2006) suggests that polygraph testing is accurate in the treatment of sex offenders, but the research is based on offender self-report. A recent evaluation of the use of polygraph testing has been undertaken by the National Probation Service. The service claims that the testing appeared to be successful and the research, involving 30 sex offenders in three areas, prevented at least three from re-offending. The sex offenders, who were all on probation, were asked a series of questions about their offending and fantasies. They were questioned about contact with children or if they had been targeting potential victims. The polygraphs measured physical response to these questions, including heart rate, blood pressure and perspiration, to establish if offenders were lying and to measure progress on the treatment programme. A more recent Home Office pilot including 350 offenders on community sentences and parole suggests that 44 per cent (214 of 347) were found to be deceptive. The respondents had volunteered to participate in the study (Home Office, 2006). Provision for compulsory polygraph testing of sex offenders sentenced to 12 months or more in custody, and who are released on licence, will be made in the Management of Offenders and Sentencing Bill (House of Lords, 2005; Home Office, 2006).[3]

There has been a considerable amount of criticism regarding the accuracy of polygraph testing, which is used routinely in the United States in risk assessment with dangerous offenders. A recent article in the *New York Times* claims that such testing has been used to assess re-offending following release, and is used in civil commitment centres to evaluate admissions about previous offending. The article claims that such is the concern in the United States regarding the accuracy of the testing that results remain inadmissible as evidence in court (currently the situation in the UK also) and that offenders

---

3   MPs voted in favour of passing the Offender Management Bill at its third reading in the House of Commons at the beginning of March 2007.

who are accustomed to lying and feel no remorse, such as psychopaths, can easily falsify the test (Goodnough and Davey 2007). However, on a more positive note, some practitioners in the United States have suggested that regardless of the accuracy of polygraph testing its use may encourage offenders to be more truthful about their behaviour (California Coalition on Sexual Offending, 2004).

In the UK the NSPCC voiced concerns regarding the introduction of polygraph testing and questioned how far human rights issues had been considered should tests become mandatory. Potential problems include: the accuracy of testing; the degree of standardisation; the extent and nature of tester training; the possible use of test results as a basis of sentencing decisions in future (NSPCC, 2006); similar questions have been posed by government ministers. In 2004 the polygraph testing of sex offenders was first proposed by the Home Secretary (David Blunkett) based upon the US model – in a letter dated 20 July, cabinet approval for the legislation, which 'requires sex offenders to undergo polygraph testing', was sought. The letter was addressed to John Prescott, the Deputy Prime Minister, as chair of the cabinet's domestic affairs committee. The cabinet expressed reservations and requested further evidence regarding the accuracy of testing. Liberty has also expressed concerns regarding the accuracy of the tests but has stated it has no objections to use, as long as test results do not form the basis of evidence in sentencing (Institute of Mental Health Law Forum, 2004). The debate is ongoing, but it seems that polygraph testing will be widely used by the National Probation Service in England and Wales soon.

Newspaper coverage of lie detector testing has been considerable over the last three years. In 2004 the press reflected upon the US experience. The *Guardian* questioned the accuracy and reliability of lie detectors, claiming that US critics believed it to be easy to deceive the test. The newspaper cites a polygraph tester in the United States who states that the accuracy of the test is based upon an assumption that certain physical reactions always accompany lying: perspiring and increased heart rate, for example. The tester claims that this is not always the case, particularly when those tested are accomplished liars (*Guardian*, 28 May 2004).

More recent coverage of the proposed introduction of polygraph testing for sex offenders has been sceptical that the Home Office is attempting to recover from the fallout following a number of highly publicised recent cases, involving early release from prison, re-offending and the failure to imprison two sex offenders due to prison overcrowding. In January 2007 a *Daily Mail* headline read 'Sex Offenders to be Given Lie Tests'. The paper went on to suggest that the Home Secretary (John Reid) was anxious to restore his public image following criticism regarding prison overcrowding. The *Daily Mirror* was less critical of the government, and appeared to support the concept of lie detector testing: 'True Life Saver: Ministers should seriously consider giving lie-detector tests to released paedophiles' (15 November 2006). The *Sun* also appeared to support the introduction of the tests with fairly uncritical coverage:

> Paedo Lie Tests 'Long Overdue' – Paedos are to face lie detector tests for the first time in the UK to see if they're likely to attack again, the Government announced last week. Sex offenders on probation will be hooked up to machines and quizzed – just like in the US. It's hoped the trials will help reduce the risk of child sex beasts wriggling past parole boards only to abuse more youngsters.
>
> (2 February 2007)

Assessing risk: a precise science or a shot in the dark?

Following ongoing media criticism and a number of cases involving early release and serious re-offending, the assessment of 'risk' has become a serious business pursued by criminal justice agencies. The assessment, measurement, management and control of the 'risky' offender are of paramount importance, and have become key indicators of prison and probation effectiveness. Risk assessment and management of sex offenders occurs at several levels – there is clearly a need for criminal justice organisations to attempt to control and manage this group of offenders via MAPPA arrangements, but police, social work and probation practitioners have the difficult task of attempting to make assessment at an individual and treatment-group level. Organisations such as the National Probation Service provide practitioners with general guidance on risk,[4] and suggest that

---

4   The Home Office 'Risk Management Framework' identifies four rather obvious steps for practitioners: 1 Identify risks; 2 Assess risks; 3 Address risk responses; 4 Risk review and report (Home Office, 2004, p 10).

probation officers should be addressing risk at every stage of the process from pre-sentence report to sentence completion. The guidance identifies four strategic objectives that should guide probation work with all sex offenders.

Probation officers are instructed to follow specific guidance in judging risk at pre-sentence report stage and making sentencing recommendations. Officers are told to consider:

- the gravity of the offence;
- how far risk can be contained within the community;
- if conditions should be added to the community sentence to address risk, e.g., residence conditions;
- if there is a need for a Sex Offence Prevention Order (Sexual Offences Act 2003) or a Disqualification Order (Criminal Justice Act 2003);
- if there is a need for an 'extended' sentence (Crime and Disorder Act 2001).

(National Probation Service, 2004)

In Scotland, risk assessment of dangerous offenders is recognised as a key issue that is monitored by a central body (the Risk Management Authority (RMA)) and is becoming an integral and structured element of practice that is monitored by a central body. This is an unusual approach. A statutory obligation is now placed upon criminal justice agencies working with violent and sexual offenders in Scotland subject to an order of lifelong restriction (OLR) to prepare and act upon a risk management plan approved and held by the RMA. The plan must include an assessment of risk and

---

1   'Timely assessment using evidence based tools'.

2   'Interventions to reduce risk'.

3   'Interventions to manage risk'.

4   'Developing accommodation options commensurate to the assessed risk'.

Figure 5.1 Probation strategic objectives
Source: National Probation Service, 2004

describe how the perceived risk will be monitored and how the offender will be managed by all relevant agencies.

The OLR formed part of the recommendations by the MacLean Committee on serious violent and sexual offenders (2000), and has been made available to the High Court, since June 2006, for offenders appearing on indictment for an offence without a mandatory life sentence of imprisonment. The statutory provisions for the OLR are set out in section 210F of the Criminal Procedure (Scotland) Act 1995 (as inserted by section 1 of the Criminal Justice (Scotland) Act 2003). The MacLean Committee also recommended establishing an independent body to ensure that statutory, voluntary and private sector agencies work together systematically to address the risk posed by serious offenders: the proposal led to the establishment of the RMA. It is the role of the RMA to approve and monitor the risk management plans prepared by agencies for those offenders serving an OLR. The authority's remit also includes: setting standards and accrediting risk assessors and the methods to be used in the assessment of those offenders for whom the court is considering an OLR; the development of policy and conduct of research in the fields of risk assessment and management; and the provision of guidance and training for criminal justice agencies and practitioners. In essence the establishment of the RMA constituted an attempt to inform the risk debate in Scotland, but also to control the way in which criminal justice practitioners assess and manage serious offenders.

In England and Wales the National Offender Management Service (NOMS) fulfils a similar function to the RMA in Scotland, but exercises less direct control over risk assessment and management of offenders by the Probation and Prison Services. There are nine NOMS regions in England and Wales; in each of the NOMS regions there is a regional offender manager who is responsible for overseeing the management of services offered by service providers in that area. The responsibility for re-offending in that area rests with the regional managers, whose responsibility it is to: commission services for their region; develop a regional reducing re-offending delivery plan; and coordinate regional and local partnerships.

NOMS seeks to encourage agencies to work together in 'end-to-end offender management' (Home Office, 2007) throughout an offenders' sentence. A new offender management model was introduced to encourage such inter-agency collaboration – the model rests upon the concept of the four Cs:

- Continuity
- Consistency
- Commitment
- Consolidation.

(Home Office, NOMS website, 2007)

The model encourages all members of a local offender management team to work together in risk assessing, managing and treating offenders to ensure continuity and consistency of approach. This is underpinned by agency commitment and consolidation. An offender management team is comprised of an offender manager, offender supervisor, key workers and case administrators. In terms of risk assessment the guiding NOMS principle in the National Offender Management Model is that 'resources follow risk' (Home Office, NOMS website, 2007). Risk is assessed using the Offender Assessment System (OASys). NOMS powers will be extended under the new Offender Management Bill.[5]

There are a number of validated risk assessment tools in use by criminal justice practitioners in the UK, the United States and Canada. These include screening tools such as OASys (favoured by the Home Office and NOMS) and Risk Matrix 2000 (RM2000) (Thornton et al. 2003), and a number of structured professional tools such as the Risk of Sexual Violence Protocol (Hart et al., 2003). OASys measures dynamic risk factors, and claims to be able to measure the impact of changes in life circumstances; it focuses upon risk of harm and risk of reconviction. Harm is categorised at three levels (low, medium and high); this informs allocation to the level of seriousness under the MAPPA arrangements. RM2000 is a risk measurement tool that was designed specifically to assess risk in all sex offenders[6] – it is an evidence-based actuarial risk assessment instrument. There has been some criticism of the ability of RM2000 to accurately predict sexual re-offending at an individual level. It has been suggested that the addition of other factors associated with re-offending, such as a

5   The Offender Management Bill has passed successfully through its third reading in the House of Commons. Under the bill, NOMS will be able to commission services from a wide range of organisations in the public, private and voluntary sectors.

6   RM2000 comprises three scales (RM2000s, RM2000v and RM2000c) which seek to predict sexual offending, violent non-sexual behaviour and sexual or other violence. Static risk factors are assessed to obtain one of four classifications: Low Risk; Medium Risk; High Risk and Very High Risk (Thornton et al., 2003).

history of employment problems, substance abuse and relationship problems, greatly enhances the ability of the scale to accurately predict risk (Craig et al., 2004). Seto (cited in Davidson, 2007) claims that most actuarial tools are competent in terms of predicting risk of re-offending but may not be adept at predicting risk of harm (to others).

Internet child sex offenders: risk assessment and management

A new category of sex offender has recently been identified, following international police operations, involving offenders using the internet to access and download indecent child images. Criminal justice agencies and the media now refer to the 'internet sex offender' as if the ever-developing technology had in some way given rise to a new form of sexual predator. Between January 2003 and January 2007 the *Daily Mail* ran approximately 50 stories on cases involving the use of the internet to sexually abuse children. Themes include inappropriately short sentences and the work of undercover police officers.

Recognition that the internet has the potential to foster the development of international child abuser rings has begun to filter through to newspaper coverage – the *Guardian*, for example, confirmed this recently in an article reporting on the detention of British offenders participating in a large, international internet sex offender ring involving over 2,000 offenders (*Guardian*, 8 February 2007). The *Daily Mail* had reported extensively on this social problem six years earlier, commenting on the discovery of the internet based 'Wonderland Club', a child-abuser ring involving 180 men operating in different countries and sharing 750,000 indecent images of children (*Daily Mail*, 12 February 2001).

The media had identified a new category of predatory sex offender and sought to actively raise public awareness around this issue, suggesting that parents should be wary about allowing their children unrestricted access to the internet. Indeed the *Daily Mirror* provided advice to parents in the form of a booklet about internet safety (Safety Net, 18 January 2007). The government and its criminal justice agencies have responded to the steady trickle of convictions for internet related child abuse through the commissioning of research in the area, by attempting to address risk and through the creation of i-SOTP in England and Wales – Scotland and Northern Ireland will probably also adopt this model.

Internet sex offenders are subject to MAPPA arrangements but are usually classified as low risk (level 1). In theory it may be easier to monitor the behaviour of this group as it may soon be possible to monitor their computer use electronically and remotely – this may initially prove costly, but such a move may provide a more cost-effective alternative in the long term than frequent MAPPA officer visits. Risk assessment techniques employed by the police and other UK agencies in work with internet sex offenders presently focuses upon the use of RM2000 (in the absence of any specific assessment tools for internet sex offenders) and the advice of SAP (2000) on classifying categories of internet offender convicted for possession of indecent images of children.[7]

The SAP system does not however extend to offenders grooming children online. Research conducted by the author indicates that the current risk assessment system has been criticised by police practitioners for being too limited and not accurately assessing risk with internet sex offenders. Internet offenders grooming children constitute a higher risk than those whose offending is limited to possessing indecent images of children – practitioners must effectively explore the real possibility that 'level 1' internet offenders are engaged in contact abuse. Although such offenders may be the exception to the rule (and this has not really been empirically established), any attempt to neatly categorise and risk-assess internet sex offenders must take into account the diversity of this offending group and the potential for contact abuse. Research into this issue has been conducted by Seto and Eke (2005a, 2005b) in Canada – the criminal records of 204 male offenders using indecent images of children[8] were analysed. The researchers suggest that offenders using indecent images of children who had committed a previous or concurrent contact sexual offence were the most likely to re-offend over a 2.5-year period (2005a). This has implications for risk assessment practice with this group. On the basis of their follow up study with 198 of the original sample of 204 male offenders, Seto and Eke (2005b) claim that criminal history is an important indicator

---

7   In terms of judging seriousness and risk when sentencing, the Court of Appeal accepted the advice of SAP (2002) in sentencing internet sex offenders using indecent images of children, following *R v Oliver, Hartrey and Baldwin*.

8   Not all of whom were internet offenders.

of risk of re-offending in offenders using indecent images of children, but that age at first charge or conviction did not seem to be a good predictive indicator of further offending. It is also suggested that risk of contact offending posed by this offender group is lower that that posed by other sex offenders. This finding should however be treated with caution. The authors acknowledge this, given the limitations of the study in terms of sample size and given that there may be differences between internet offenders using indecent images and offenders accessing such images via a different media.

Little work has been undertaken in attempting to address risk with those who target and groom children online, other than that undertaken by Strano (2004) in Rome, ongoing doctoral research with the Metropolitan Police in London (Martellozzo, 2006, unpublished) and O'Connell (2003), who spent some time in children's chat rooms posing as a child in order to engage would-be online groomers. O'Connell identifies several different stages in the online grooming process, during which an offender will seek to identify and target a potential victim, develop an online relationship with them, explore vulnerability and availability, and ultimately arrange to meet.

Research conducted by Quayle and Taylor (2002) with social workers and probation officers suggested that practitioners did not understand 'the function of the internet for adults with a sexual interest in children' (2002, p 32) and did not routinely screen sex offenders for internet use, an issue that is of concern and that was also raised by a representative from the High Technology Crime Unit of the Metropolitan Police.[9] Quayle and Taylor (2002) comment in this work that there are currently no specific assessment tools to aid practitioners in managing internet sex offenders (this has been confirmed by representatives from the Family Protection, Scotland and the National Probation Service in England and Wales, 2006). Practitioners in Quayle and Taylor's study were relying upon the standard assessment interview to make judgements about risk.

The National Probation Service Sex Offender Strategy (2004) makes reference to provision in the CJA 2003 regarding internet offending. It is clear from the document that risk assessment is considered key at various stages of the criminal justice process,

---

9   This unit is responsible for policing online child sexual abuse, including the possession, production and distribution of indecent images of children and online grooming.

but risk assessment tools for use with internet sex offenders are currently under development and advice offered to probation practitioners acknowledges the difficulty of applying RM2000 to work with this group of offenders. Practitioners are also instructed to use the Sex Offender Psychometric Scoring System (SOPSSys) to assess the treatment needs of all sex offenders (Probation Circular 92/2005).

As a society we should undoubtedly be concerned about the risk posed to children by sex offenders, and it follows that practitioner risk assessment is of paramount importance at pre-sentence report stage in informing sentencing decisions and suitability for treatment; it is equally important during sentence (in informing release decisions for custodial sentences and risk issues in the community) and post-release. Police practitioners have, however, commented upon the lack of inter-agency knowledge sharing and collaboration at the pre-sentence report stage and beyond – it has been suggested that much greater collaboration is needed between MAPPA officers and probation officers in continually assessing risk with all categories of sex offender (Davidson, 2007). The consequence of not addressing risk appropriately and effectively with this group of offenders will be high and any mistakes potentially damaging to the reputation of the agencies concerned. However, the ability to accurately predict human behaviour is highly problematic and never more so than in work with a volatile offender group; it would seem that the systems to monitor and control this group of offenders are in place but resourcing is inadequate, inter-agency communication poor and practitioner confidence in risk assessment tools low.

Treating child sexual abusers

The Probation Service has taken increasing responsibility for work in the community with sex offenders over the last 20 years – in the twenty-first century the Home Office views sex offender treatment as the cornerstone of an effective risk management approach (Home Office, 2002). Although treatment programmes for male sex offenders (there is no similar provision for female sex offenders) have developed separately in the Probation and Prison Service, provision structure and content has recently merged. The cognitive behavioural approach to treatment with sex offenders, and particularly child sexual abusers, was developed by probation practitioners during the late 1980s–early 1990s. Barker and Morgan's 1993 survey of probation practice, undertaken on behalf of the Home Office, identified 63 probation-led programmes across 55 areas (some were running several programmes), only three of which had been running for five years or more. At this time only 13 services had clear policy statements regarding work with sex offenders. The findings from this research suggested that only one-third of services ran programmes exclusively for child sexual abusers, and also suggested that such programmes were largely unsupported by the senior management of the service. A second survey suggested that by 1996 probation management had woken up to the importance of resourcing provision for 'dangerous' offenders: the number of programmes run by the service had almost doubled since 1993, and more than 50 of the then 55 areas had specific policies in place (Proctor and Flaxington, 1996). A revised Home Office-accredited programme now operates in each of the three regions that comprise the National Probation Service.

It was not until the early 1990s that the Home Office developed a central policy regarding the treatment of sex offenders in prisons. At a time when probation services were establishing therapeutic programmes for sex offenders, commentators criticised the way in which child sexual abusers were able to interact under the isolation rule (then Rule 43) – some suggested that this enabled the creation of abuser rings and sharing of deviant sexual fantasies (Glaser and Spencer, 1990). In response to such criticism the Home Office introduced the prison SOTP in 1991. The programme was based upon the existing probation cognitive behavioural model and included a short, core element and longer, more intensive element for offenders serving longer sentences. The programme was introduced to 14 prisons originally, and currently operates in 27 prisons in England and Wales.

The current community and prison treatment programme

The prison and community treatment programmes have now merged and are accredited by an independent panel – in effect this provision has been brought firmly under the control of the Home Office over the last five years and practitioners are no longer able to work in an ad hoc fashion with 'dangerous' offenders (Home Office, 2002). The programme is, however, still based on the original cognitive behavioural theoretical model developed by the Probation Service in the 1980s, which drew heavily upon David Finkelhor's (1986) 'eclectic' approach to treatment.

The term cognitive behaviour is used in this context to describe a broad approach incorporating central themes. The approach focuses upon the extent to which offenders seek to attribute blame to their victims, others and offence circumstances, rather than accepting their role in the commission of the offences. The theory has been developed further by Gudjonsson (1987, 1990, 1991), who traces its origins to early attribution theorists such as psychologist John Bowlby. Treatment here has sought to enable offenders to accept responsibility for their own behaviour, and to understand the impact that their behaviour has had upon their victim. Practical work involves the challenging of offender accounts of their offending, which are held to be inaccurate or misleading – comparisons are made here with victims' versions of events. Offenders must also participate in role play, in which they adopt the role of their victim and their victim's relatives (where appropriate). This approach also rests upon the assumption that offenders will have low self-esteem and be socially isolated individuals incapable of maintaining success-ful adult relationships. In practice, programmes seek to teach social skills, to raise confidence and to cause offenders to reflect upon the negative and positive aspects of past relationships. Programmes also aim to encourage the development of adult social activities.

The Prison Service SOTP is comprised of five inter-related group work programmes. In the Probation Service, three Sex Offender Group Programmes have been accredited: in the West Midlands (C-SOGP), Thames Valley (TV-SOGP) and Northumbria (N-SOGP). The programmes have a number of different entry points for offenders according to their level of risk and deviance, and whether they have completed a SOTP in prison. All the programmes use

---

1   Offender denial and minimisation.

2   Blame attribution: lack of victim empathy.

3   Social skill deficiency.

4   Low self-esteem.

Figure 5.2 Key treatment areas – SOTP

methods such as group discussion, role play and skills practice to help offenders understand and change their thinking, develop new skills and prepare for a new type of life. Programme content has been revised in keeping with new research developments on effectiveness. The prison and probation treatment programmes operate together. An offender attending the prison programme will be expected to attend a follow up probation programme on release from custody. The prison and probation programmes use the same risk assessment methods and have a similar modular design.

Sex offender denial and minimisation in treatment programmes

The concept of denial is central to treatment approaches with sex offenders in the UK, the United States and Canada. Treatment rests upon the assumption that even when offenders plead guilty, the consequences of offending behaviour will be denied and blame attributed to the victim, offence circumstances or internal factors beyond the individuals control. Research exploring the effectiveness of cognitive behavioural treatment programmes has sought to establish how far the concept can be supported empirically. Research undertaken by the author compared sex offender and victim accounts of offence circumstance to explore this issue (Davidson 2001, 2005).

Respondents tended to blame the offence circumstances and the victim for what were often described as momentary lapses of control. In general when asked directly about feelings regarding their behaviour the majority expressed remorse and shame:

> I feel pretty disgusted really. I always liked kids and liked being around kids. (R 1.5)

> I know it was wrong, nothing like that should have happened. (R 1.14)

> Ashamed more than anything, I should have known because she's a child she wouldn't understand what was wrong. (R 1.4)

However, when a more open interviewing approach was taken and respondents were asked to describe the offence circumstances, a somewhat different picture emerges. The respondent's versions of events were compared to the statements of their victims, where available. One respondent had been convicted for two sexual offences against children, aged seven and six. There were also allegations of sexual abuse against a third child (aged one), which were not proven. The respondent had pleaded guilty to two counts of indecent assault and had been sentenced to a three-year probation order with a psychiatric condition to attend for group treatment. All offences had been perpetrated while baby sitting for neighbours and friends. The respondent described in some detail the events leading up to the offending. The manner in which the events are described suggests that the respondent had little control over these and that the offending arose by chance:

> I became very friendly with the mother (victim's mother). She had a daughter, she was 7 or 8 I think, I spent a lot of time there baby-sitting. I was baby-sitting a lot. Q. How often? A. Several times per week. The girl's mother was married she often worked nights, she was divorced and her ex-husband wasn't interested (in the children). So I said don't worry if you cannot get a baby-sitter I will do it. She wasn't the type to ask so I volunteered, I wanted to help out. (R 1.1)

The respondent describes a situation in which help was offered to a single mother, it appeared to be his contention at this point that the offending was unplanned and arose spontaneously. In later interviews the respondent stated that he had deliberately selected and targeted the victim as the circumstances appeared ideal to perpetrate abuse. This is consistent with other research, which has suggested that offenders spend a considerable amount of time planning offences and targeting vulnerable victims (Salter, 1988).

The respondent also suggested that the victim enjoyed the abuse perpetrated; the victim statement contradicts this contention, the victim reports feeling scared of the respondent when the abuse was occurring and also states that the abuse caused her pain. The victim goes on to describe the abuse as 'horrible' and as 'making me feel sick'. This finding is consistent with research, which suggests that perpetrators of sexual offences against children justify offending behaviour with reference to feelings of love towards children and by claiming that children are sexually responsive, provocative beings. Abel and Becker, in their 1984 study of abusers attending a treatment programme in the United States, claim that offenders typically believed that a demonstration of affection towards an adult on the part of a child indicates that the child wishes to have sex with that adult and that sexually abusing children was a demonstration of love for the child on their part. Some respondents suggested that their behaviour would not damage the children concerned. 'I didn't think I was doing any wrong (R 1.1).'

Coupled with this was the belief that the behaviour was acceptable. Victim statements contradict this contention. They suggest that, rather than willing accomplices to abuse, children were in fear of perpetrators and disturbed by their behaviour. On this theme, respondents were asked if their victims had any choice but to participate – most believed that they did:

> She (victim) wasn't unhappy or resistant. All she had to do was get up and go, I wouldn't have stopped her. (R 1.6)

> I didn't force her, she seemed to enjoy it. (R 1.12)

Research has demonstrated that the loss of control in sexually abusive relationships with adults and fear of being harmed by the perpetrator, frequently prevents children from responding to the abuse at the time and from reporting abuse (Salter, 1988).

Gudjonsson (1990, 1991) discusses the manner in which blame is attributed by offenders, referring to internal and external attribution. Internal attribution occurs when blame is attributed to internal factors, such as the offender's state of mind, and external attribution occurs when external factors, such as the offence circumstances or victim behaviour, are blamed for the offending behaviour. Groth et al. (1982) have developed classifications for child abusers that have been adopted in treatment programmes. He distinguishes between fixated abusers, who are unable to build and maintain adult relationships, and regressed abusers, who retreat into relationships with children when adult relationships break down.

The literature on denial is supported by the findings from interviews undertaken with sex offenders by the author, which indicated that offenders were denying of the consequences of their behaviour upon the victim, and to an extent their own responsibility in perpetrating the act (Abel and Becker, 1984, 1987). Offenders demonstrated a tendency to minimise the consequences of the behaviour upon their victims and their families. In contrast the victims, many of whom were still children when interviewed by the police, described feelings of fear and hopelessness, using words such as 'scared', 'angry' and 'frightened' to describe their feelings towards the perpetrator.

Treating internet sex offenders

Quayle and Taylor (2003) have developed a Cognitive Behavioural Treatment (CBT) Module for internet sex offenders along with the NSPCC and Greater Manchester Probation Service. The module sought to build upon the accredited probation SOTP in guiding practitioners' work with internet sex offenders. Elements of the module will be used in the new accredited Home Office probation programme for internet sex offenders, which has been developed by Middleton (2006, cited in Davidson, 2007). The i-SOTP programme was accredited by the Correctional Services Accreditation Panel in December 2005 and probation staff have been trained in its use. Intervention staff run the accredited offender management programmes and often have specialist experience/knowledge in the sex offender area.

The theoretical basis of the programme draws upon a number of sources including Quayle's original internet CBT module; the spiral of abuse model; and Finkelhor's 'multi-factoral' approach (1984) upon which the original SOTP was based. The programme is restricted to offenders categorised as 'low deviance' in terms of RM2000 (MAPPA level 1). The implication is that although the programme has been designed for those convicted of indecent image related offending, the content and structure of the programme should allow for the allocation of different types of internet sex offender to different and appropriate treatment streams. For example, the effective management of online groomers may require more one-to-one supervision, along with elements of the original SOTP and i-SOTP. However, information produced for practitioners by the National Probation Directorate (Probation Circular 92/2005) indicates that the programme has been designed exclusively for 'offenders who have been convicted of offences which involved the viewing, making, possession, distribution of indecent images of children through the medium of electronic communication' (2005, p 2).

Elsewhere there appear to be few treatment programmes dedicated to internet sex offenders, other than small scale, ad hoc projects largely developed by practitioners. In Switzerland, for example, 40 internet sex offenders have undergone a tailored CBT programme (Interview, Graf, 2006, cited in Davidson, 2007) and some work is underway in the Netherlands at the Amsterdam Clinic. There is work in the UK to address risk assessment and treatment for internet sex offenders who possess, produce and distribute indecent images of children,[10] most notably that undertaken by O'Brien and Webster (2005, unpublished) on behalf of the UK Prison Service Offending Behaviour Programmes Unit, and developmental work conducted by Middleton et al. (2005, in press) on behalf of the National Probation Service – these developments are discussed below.

Middleton et al. (2005) conducted research exploring the applicability of the Ward and Siegert Pathways Model of Sexual Offending to a sample of 72 internet sex offenders who had been convicted for possession and distribution of indecent images of children. The sample was drawn from the National Probation Service in England and Wales – 67 per cent (*n* = 49) of the sample had been risk assessed using RM2000; 17 per cent had been categorised as high risk.

What do we know about child abusers using the internet? Middleton et al. suggest that internet sex offenders are a diverse group – this is confirmed by O'Brien and Webster's (2005) work, which found that some of these offenders have similar psychological problems to other sex offenders. The implications for assessment and treatment are that risk assessment tools and treatment should take account of these differences, and the cognitive behavioural treatment approach adopted by both the Probation and Prison Service with sex offenders in the UK at present may not be entirely relevant. This contention is however contradicted by the work of O'Brien and Webster (2005), whose research was conducted with internet sex offenders. O'Brien and Webster sought to design and validate a risk assessment measure to guide the work of practitioners. Their Internet Behaviour and Attitudes Questionnaire (IBAQ, 2006) draws upon Quayle and Taylor's (2003) interview guidelines for practitioners in work with internet sex offenders. Other items on the scale were developed following a literature review and interviews with the Metropolitan Police. The IBAQ contains a series of 42 behaviour-related items that require a 'yes/no' response and 34 attitude items.

---

10 None of this research has focused upon those who groom children online, possibly as there are currently few such offenders in the system and cases are difficult and time consuming to evidence

The questions explore the nature of the offender's internet behaviour in relation to indecent child images and general attitudes towards internet abuse. Many of these statements seek to explore denial and minimisation regarding the seriousness and extent of the behaviour – these concepts are well established in treatment work with sex offenders and evidenced in the general sex offender literature (Finkelhor, 1984; Gudjonsson, 1991; Davidson, 2005).

O'Brien and Webster's research was divided into two phases: 40 sexual offenders with a history of using indecent images participated in phase one (pilot) and 123 sexual offenders convicted of internet child pornography participated in the second phase. All respondents were serving custodial or probation sentences. The internal consistency of the measure used with phase two respondents increased following changes made as a consequence of data produced at phase one. The IBAQ may shortly be used in the new CBT development by Middleton (2006). The authors do however caution that the scale does not yet have the capability to accurately measure risk. On a more optimistic note, it is suggested that elements of the CBT treatment model currently in use for sex offenders may have some relevance for internet sex offenders, but in the absence of any conclusive empirical evidence this conclusion must be tentative.

- Intimacy and social skills deficit

- Distorted sexual scripts

- Anti-social cognitions

- Emotional dysregulation

- Cognitive distortions:
  1 Justification of possession (only an image)
  2 Normalisation (many others do this)
  3 Objectification of victim/victims
  4 Collusion (with wider network).

Figure 5.3 Key treatment areas guiding work with internet sex offenders using indecent child images

Source: Middleton, 2006 (cited in Davidson, 2007)

Research undertaken by the author suggests that some practitioners are sceptical about the benefits of developing a tailored programme for internet sex offenders given the developmental state of knowledge and research on internet sexual abuse:

> I'm not sure we have enough knowledge yet to devise a specific programme for internet sex offenders. Do we know enough about what is different about sex offenders who use the internet in the commission of their offending? It seems quite possible that they are more similar than different from the population of contact offenders we already work with.
>
> (R 6, Davidson, 2007)

This concern was shared to a certain extent by a probation officer delivering the new i-SOTP programme, who commented that although the 'internet offenders' attending the programme had been convicted for indecent child image related offences, some had previous convictions for contact sexual abuse and many were using the internet in other areas of their lives; to build other adult relationships, for example, and to approach children in chat rooms. Another CBT treatment programme is currently operational at a local level at the Forensic Department of University Hospital in Basel, Switzerland. This inpatient and outpatient clinic for sex offenders includes those remanded in custody; on probation; post-release from prison; and some self-referring (approximately 15–20 per cent of all internet offenders are self referring). Forty men have attended the programme so far; therapy lasts for one year (weekly sessions of 1.5 hours) and is based upon relapse prevention models adapted for use with internet sex offenders. The majority of offenders have been charged with possession of child internet pornography. The programme has been running for four years, and the CBT model used is based upon the work of Marshall, Laws and Barbaree (1990), which has been adapted for use with sex offenders using indecent internet images of children (Graf, 2006). A different approach to risk assessment is employed by Graf, and actuarial assessment tools are not favoured.

Risk assessment and management will be an integral element of the new i-SOTP programme – probation offender managers and facilitators must currently produce approved risk plans. Standard training materials for trainers are currently under development, as is a standardised internet sex offender test battery which will be used by the Prison Service and the National Probation Service (across all probation regions). This is similar to the psychometric test battery currently used for SOTP. Much treatment practice with internet sex offenders is new and innovative; the effectiveness of different approaches will not be apparent until the work has progressed sufficiently to allow for the collection of data and evaluation. Many criminal justice and social work agencies are attempting to build upon existing good practice in terms of assessment and treatment for sex offenders and to adapt this practice for use with sex offenders whose offences are internet related.

Although practitioners are dedicated and much of the work is innovative, it is essential that good quality research underpins practice; there is a scarcity of such research regarding the behaviour of different types of internet sex offender (Quayle and Taylor's (2003) and Krone's (2004) work is the exception). Research has focused upon those who produce and collect indecent images of children, while very little is known about those who groom children online, for example, and the boundary between online abuse and contact abuse (if such a boundary exists). The police have suggested that a greater number of online grooming cases are now being prosecuted under the Sexual Offences Act 2003.

Treatment evaluation

The Probation Service has been criticised for its continued use of the cognitive behavioural approach, and for promoting the belief that this constitutes the most effective treatment method (Mair, 2000). The extent to which offender-behaviour programmes have achieved their goal is usually measured with reference to reconviction data. However, the extent to which the rate of reconviction is indicative of levels of offending, particularly where offending is hidden and victims unlikely to disclose abuse, is questionable. It could be that treated sex offenders become more socially skilled and more able to avoid detection than untreated offenders. Research indicates that reconviction rates for untreated sex offenders are considerably higher than for treated sex offenders. Hedderman and Sugg (1996) found that offenders receiving an ordinary probation order were five times more likely to be reconvicted over a six-year period than offenders attending a probation treatment programme, while Proctor and Flaxington (1997) have suggested that untreated sex offenders were three times more likely to be reconvicted over a five-year period.

Friendship, Mann and Beech's 2003 evaluation of SOTP found a lower rate of reconviction for untreated sex offenders (committing further sexual offences) in a two-year follow up, but cautiously acknowledge that the findings are not statistically significant and point to difficulties associated with the validity of reconviction rates as an indicator of programme effectiveness. Research incorporating reconviction rates does, however, show a distinct difference. Marshall et al. (1990) in their earlier United States study followed a sample of 126 treated and untreated child sexual abusers attending one clinic over a one- to two-year period. The research subjects were divided into the following categories: men abusing non-familial girls; men abusing non-familial boys; and incest abusers. The non-familial abusers were generally more likely to re-offend (or perhaps to be caught re-offending) than were the incest abusers. In all three categories the untreated abusers were much more likely to re-offend than were the treated offenders. Even allowing for the difficulties associated with the use of reconviction data, the findings show a marked difference between those receiving treatment and those not receiving treatment. It should, however, be noted that no reference is made by the authors to the number of offenders in the treatment group completing the treatment programme.

What makes for successful treatment? This is difficult to answer with any certainty, but key variables such as offender motivation to change (Briggs and Kennington, 2006) and group-leader style seem to be important. Marshall et al. (2003), in their recent research for the Prison Service, suggest that group-leader style is key in producing positive treatment outcomes with sex offenders – they observed videoed sessions from SOTP and concluded that a confrontational group-leader style may have a negative outcome. Research conducted by the author with two groups of convicted child sexual abusers suggests that those experiencing a more confrontational approach were more negative about the impact of the treatment than those experiencing a more interactive, less confrontational approach (Davidson, 2001). Beckett et al. (1994) have suggested that an over-controlling leadership style is detrimental to the development of group cohesion.

The motivation to change and recognition that behaviour is problematic may be key indicators in predicting successful treatment outcomes with this group. Evaluation of the prison programme by Beech et al. (1998) suggests that offenders who failed to accept responsibility for their behaviour were more likely to re-offend, as were those undertaking the shorter, less intensive programme. These variables may also be important in predicting risk of re-offending, but it is clear that quantifying them may prove problematic. A recent development, which has been funded by the Home Office, is known as 'circles of support and accountability'. Here volunteers provide support and help to sex offenders who are isolated in the community and recently released from custody. The scheme is based on Quaker principles, and aims to help foster confidence and self-esteem and encourage independence, helping offenders to overcome the desire to offend. The volunteers are trained and take on a mentoring role, and will meet with offenders when they need support – a contract is drawn up between the offender and the volunteer which is based upon the offender's needs. The scheme is based on work in Canada and has begun to spread in the UK (Quaker website, 2007). The schemes are yet to be evaluated but may provide isolated offenders with much-needed support on leaving custody and in facing society.

Recent trends: offence disclosure and chemical castration

Public disclosure: one step closer?

Media and public pressure upon the government to disclose sex offender details has become considerable in the wake of the Sarah Payne and Soham cases. The Home Office has recently undertaken a review in this area (6/2007) and plans to legislate to introduce a watered down version of the system that operates in the United States following the introduction of Megan's Law. The proposed legislation will place a legal obligation upon MAPPA agencies (including the Probation Service and the police) to consider disclosure of information to the public about sex offenders in *all* cases. The disclosure decision will be based upon the offender's perceived risk to children. This move effectively endows MAPPA agencies with the power to disclose, effectively removing the decision from sentencers and the Home Office. The basis on which such decisions should be taken is not discussed in the document, but will presumably rest in part upon existing risk assessment tools, such as RM2000 and practitioner assessment. Action Three in the review states that the government plan to:

> introduce a legal duty for MAPPA authorities to consider the disclosure of information about convicted child sex offenders to

members of the public in all cases. The presumption will be that the authorities will disclose information if they consider that an offender presents a risk of serious harm to a member of the publics children (p 13).

The new legislation will also allow a member of the public to register a child protection interest against someone who has previous convictions for sexual offences against children, and the police may disclose this information to a 'relevant' member of the public. This may occur, for example, where an individual with previous convictions becomes involved with a family who have children, but who are unaware of the person's past. A concerned friend or neighbour may register a child protection interest and the police will have a duty to investigate the basis of the claim and possibly inform the family.

It is clear from the review that the Home Office is attempting to gain public support for such measures through greater community engagement under MAPPA arrangements. Just how this might function in practice is unclear. The review also stresses the need to strengthen MAPPA arrangements.

The use of drugs to control sex offender behaviour

Drugs have been used in an attempt to control sex offender behaviour, in the UK, in other European countries such as France and the Netherlands, in the United States and in Canada for some time. This procedure is often referred to as 'chemical castration' and involves the use of testosterone reducing anti-androgen drugs, administered to control sexual desire. The drugs are synthetic progestins which inhibit hormone development and limit development of testosterone. Craissati (2004) suggests that the use of drugs such as Cyproterone Acetate (CPA), which is licenced for use in Europe and Canada, and Medroxyprogesterone acetate (MPA), licenced for use in the United States, results in sperm reduction, loss of sexual desire and frustration. Weiss (1999) has speculated that chemical castration allows offenders to focus upon treatment rather than offending, but there is no research evidence to support this claim. Cumming and Buell (1997) claim that offenders are still able to maintain an erection, have sexual intercourse and ejaculate while taking the drugs.

In France chemical castration has been piloted with a small group of 48 sex offenders who have served custodial sentences and agreed to participate in a drugs trial on release from custody. The study will explore the impact upon reconviction rates. The findings from this work have yet to be published (BBC News, 13 January 2005). It has been suggested that this move is an attempt to address the increasing rate of reported child sexual abuse in France; a German broadcaster claims that almost 25 per cent of male offenders in French prisons are sex offenders and that approximately 75 per cent of these have perpetrated offences against children (Laurensen, 2005). Lameyre (2000) suggests that convictions for rape in France doubled from 1984 to 1997; the state response to this has been the introduction of more punitive legislation for sex offenders and considerably longer custodial sentences.

Other European countries using chemical castration include Belguim, Italy, Germany, Denmark, Hungary and Sweden. In Denmark offenders were offered surgical castration as an alternative to prison up until 1970, but chemical castration is now offered. In Sweden the intervention is offered on a voluntary basis. There is little research addressing the effectiveness of this approach and such work stresses the importance of using drug control in the context of counselling/treatment. Research conducted by Hansen and Lykke-Olesen (1997) in Denmark suggests that sex offenders responded positively to drug intervention over time and were less likely to re-offend, although it is extremely difficult to measure rates of re-offending.

There are several problems associated with drug trials research in this area. First, reconviction rates are not valid indicators of re-offending, particularly in sex offender populations where offending is frequently hidden and, second, there is the possibility of a 'research effect', offenders may control their behaviour in the knowledge that they are participating in the trial and being monitored. Another is that offender samples are very small and probably unrepresentative. The findings from such work are at best inconclusive.

In the United States compulsory chemical castration was introduced for sex offenders in California on 17 September 1996.[11] This

---

11 See *Constitutional Law. Due Process and Equal Protection. California Becomes First State to Require Chemical Castration of Certain Sex Offenders*. Act of Sept 17 1996, ch 596, 1996 Cal Stat 92 (To Be Codified at Cal Penal Code, section 645) *Harvard Law Review*, 110(3) (Jan 1997), pp 799–804 doi:10.2307/1342251.

legislation required the court to sentence any repeat child abuser whose victim was under 13-years-old to drugs treatment, and allowed sentencers discretion in using drugs for other sex offenders abusing children. Similar legislation was enacted in Florida six months later (Helm Spalding, 1998). Consequently all repeat sex offenders (where the victim is under 13) must agree to take drugs as a condition of release from prison. Compliance with the intervention is monitored via the taking of regular blood samples. Chemical castration is compulsory in other states such as Florida, Washington, Michigan and Texas. The American Civil Liberties Union (ACLU) opposed the use of chemical castration in 1997, describing the intervention as a 'cruel and unusual punishment' (Helm Spalding, 1997) and therefore unacceptable under the US Bill of Rights. This term is taken from the Eighth Amendment to the United States Constitution, which states that *cruel and unusual punishments shall not be used* (1787) (Bill of Rights, US House of Representatives National Archives, 2007). This claim was unsuccessful and did not prevent the introduction of chemical castration in other US states. The ACLU also claimed that the drugs would interfere with offender's right to procreate.

It has been claimed that the move to introduce chemical castration in California was never supported by the medical profession, and that the intervention is only effective with offenders motivated to change their behaviour (Berlin, 1997). The Association for the Treatment of Sexual Abusers (ATSA) in the United States does not support the widespread use of drugs in controlling sex offender behaviour. In a position paper on the use of anti-androgen therapy, ATSA states that its use should be limited given individual differences. It is recommended that such drugs should be prescribed by a doctor following an extensive period of evaluation of individual need; there should be ongoing medical supervision due to the possible harmful side effects; administration should occur in the context of a treatment plan (this is usually not the case in the United States) and that an offender's informed consent to the administration of such drugs should always be gained (ATSA, 2007). This point is supported by Harrison (2007) in the UK who recently conducted a literature review exploring the advantages and disadvantages of chemical castration. This is also clearly not the case in the aforementioned states where chemical castration is a compulsory element of release from prison.

The use of drugs to control offending behaviour has been criticised on ethical grounds in the light of possible harmful side effects which can include for example: insomnia; depression; hypoglycaemia; blood clots; allergic reactions; diabetes; breast enlargement; damaged liver, and weight gain (Berlin and Manicke, 1981; Craissati, 2004). Some have suggested that the side effects are particularly pronounced in adolescent sex offenders (Gagne, 1981). The drugs have only recently been used in this way and consequently there is no research exploring the long-term effects. The employment of drugs to suppress sexual desire assumes that the act of child abuse is entirely physiological; this is a misconception. Research demonstrates that child abusers enjoy the company of children; enjoy the feeling of power, control and domination that the abuse of a child affords; are likely to have experienced abuse and rejection in past relationships, and have low self-esteem (Finkelhor, 1984; Davidson, 2001). The forces that drive an individual to abuse a child are highly complex and not always necessarily predicated only upon sexual desire, a point made by Helm Spalding (1997) opposing the initial intro-duction of chemical castration in California. It is also apparent that only those individuals motivated to change are likely to benefit. The government are undoubtedly attempting to assuage public outcry through the introduction of a range of measures, for which there is very little conclusive research evidence to suggest effectiveness. This would seem to be an attempt to find a 'quick fix' simple solution to a very complex issue.

The responsibility of 'protecting the public from serious harm' posed by child sexual abusers in the real world and in cyberspace is a difficult one; such offences are shrouded in secrecy; offenders often effectively conceal abuse; victims are often reluctant to report abuse and consequently offences are under reported. Attempts to control, manage, treat and predict re-offending are fraught with difficulties, and any mistakes involving the commission of further sexual offences against children will be played out in the full glare of the media spotlight. Practitioners working with such difficult offenders are charged with the responsibility of accurately predicting the risk they pose and with their rehabilitation. This work occurs in the context of MAPPA arrangements and measures, such as polygraph testing and satellite tracking, introduced by the Home Office to place restrictions upon sex offender's behaviour in the community.

Key chapter themes

- The government has introduced a range of measures to attempt to monitor and control the movements of child sexual abusers in the community including the proposed use of drugs and polygraph testing.

- The introduction of such measures has occurred in the face of ongoing media criticism regarding the mis-management of sex offenders in the community and a number of cases involving early release from custody and re-offending.

- Policy guiding work with dangerous offenders now focuses upon the assessment of risk, the effective management of child sexual abusers, and standardised probation and prison treatment programmes.

References

Abel, G C and Becker, J V, 'The treatment of child molesters', *Treatment Manual* (1984), unpublished

Abel, G C and Becker, J V, 'Self reported sex crimes of non-incarcerated paraphilliacs', *Journal of Interpersonal Violence*, 2(6) (1987), pp 3–25

Association for the Treatment of Sexual Abusers, 'Position statement: Anti-androgen therapy and surgical castration', 7, 1997, accessed May 2007, www.atsa.com/ppanianto.html

Barker, M and Morgan R, *Sex Offenders: A Framework for the Evaluation of Community Based Treatment*, 1993, London: Home Office

BBC News 'French test "chemical castration"', 13 January 2005, http://news.bbc.co.uk/1/hi/world/europe/4170963.stm

Beckett, R C, Beech, A, Fisher, D and Fordham, A S, *Community Based Treatment for Sex Offenders: An Evaluation of Seven Treatment Programmes*, 1994, London: Home Office

Beech, A, Fisher, D, Beckett, R and Fordham, A S, 'STEP 3: An evaluation of the prison sex offender treatment programme', 1998, Home Office Research, Development and Statistics Occasional Paper, London: Home Office

Berlin, F S, 'Chemical castration for sex offenders', [Letter to the editor], *New England Journal of Medicine*, 336(14) (April 1997), p 1030

Berlin, F S and Menicke, C F, 'Treatment of sex offenders with antiandrogen medication: Conceptualization, review of treatment modalities and preliminary findings', *American Journal of Psychiatry*, 138 (1981), pp 601–7

Bill of Rights, United States House of Representatives National Archives, 2007, accessed July 2007, www.archives.gov/national-archives-experience/charters/bill_of_rights_transcript.html

Briggs, D and Kennington, R, *Managing Men Who Sexually Abuse*, 2006, London: Jessica Kingsley

California Coalition on Sexual Offending, 'Position paper for clinical polygraph examinations in treating sex offenders', 2004, accessed January 2007, http://216.239.59.104/search?q=cache:czr-vPhja2QJ:ccoso.org/papers/polygraphdraft.pdf+Polygraph+testing+sex+offenders+research&hl=en&ct=clnk&cd=15&gl=uk&client=firefox-a

'Constitutional law, due process and equal protection: California becomes first state to require chemical castration of certain sex offenders', *Harvard Law Review*, 110(3) (1997), pp 799–804

Craig, L, Browne, K and Beech, A, 'Identifying sexual and violent re-offenders', British Psychological Society Conference, Division of Forensic Psychology, 22 March 2004, Leicester University

Craissati, J, *Managing High Risk Sex Offenders in the Community: A Psychological Approach*, 2004, New York: Routledge

Cumming, G and Buell, M, *Supervision of the Sex Offender*, 1997, Brandon, VT: Safer Society Press

Davidson, J, 'The context and practice of community treatment programmes for convicted child sexual abusers in England and Wales', unpublished PhD thesis, 2001, London School of Economics and Political Science

Davidson, J, 'Victims speak: Comparing child sexual abusers and child victims accounts, perceptions and interpretations of sexual abuse', *Victims and Offenders*, 1(2) (2005), pp 159–74

Davidson, J, 'Current practice and research into internet sex offending', 2007, Risk Management Authority (Scotland)

Finkelhor, D, *Child Sexual Abuse: New Theory and Research*, 1984, New York: Free Press

Finkelhor, D, Araji, S, Baron, L, Browne, A, Doyle-Peters, S and Wyatt, G E, *A Sourcebook on Child Sexual Abuse*, 1986, California: Sage

Friendship, T, Mann, R and Beech, A, *The Prison Based Sex Offender Treatment Programme: An Evaluation*, 2003, London: Home Office

Gagne, P, 'Treatment of sex offenders with medroxyprogesterone acetate', *American Journal of Psychiatry*, 138 (1981), pp 644–6

Glaser, D and Spencer, J, 'Sentencing, children's evidence and trauma', *Criminal Law Review*, 3 (1990), pp 380–95

Goodnough, A and Davey, M, 'For sex offenders, dispute on therapy's benefits', *New York Times*, 6 March 2007

Groth, N A, Longo, R E and McFadin, J B, 'Undetected recidivism in rapists and child molesters', *Crime and Delinquency*, 28 (1982), pp 450–8

Grubin, D, 'Accuracy and utility of post-conviction polygraph testing of sex offenders', *The British Journal of Psychiatry*, 188 (2006), pp 479–83

Gudjonsson, G, 'The revised Gudjonsson blame attribution inventory', *Personal Individual Differences*, 10(1) (1987), pp 67–70

Gudjonsson, G, 'Self deception and other deception in forensic assessment', *Personal Individual Differences*, 11(3) (1990), pp 219–25

Gudjonsson, G, 'The attribution of blame and type of crime committed: Transcultural validation', *Journal of Forensic Science Society*, 31(3) (1991), pp 349–52

Hansen, H and Lykke-Olesen, L, 'Treatment of dangerous sexual offenders in Denmark', *Journal of Forensic Psychiatry*, 8(1) (1997), pp 195–9

Harrison, K, 'The high-risk sex offender strategy in England and Wales: Is chemical castration an option?' *Howard Journal*, 46(1) (February 2007), pp 16–31

Hart, S D, Kropp, P K, Laws, D R, Klaver, J, Logan, C and Watt, K A, *The Risk for Sexual Violence*, 2003, Mental Health, Law and Policy Institute, Vancouver, Canada: Simon Fraser University

Hedderman, C and Sugg, D, *Does Treating Sex Offenders Reduce Re-offending?*, Research Findings No 45, 1996, London: Home Office

Helm Spalding, L, 'Chemical castration: A return to the Dark Ages', American Civil Liberties Union, August 1997, accessed January 2007, www.aclufl.org/about/newsletters/1997/chem.cfm

Helm Spalding, L, 'Florida's 1997 chemical castration law: A return to the Dark Ages', Florida State University Law Review, 1998, accessed January 2007, www.law.fsu.edu/journals/lawreview/frames/252/spalfram.html

Home Office, *Protecting the Public: Strengthening Protection Against Sex Offenders and Reforming the Law on Sexual Offences*, 2002, Home Office: London

Home Office, *Risk Management and Policy Strategy: A Guide for Probation Areas and NPD*, 2004, London: HMSO

Home Office, 'Regulatory impact assessment: Making provision in the management of offenders and sentencing bill for the mandatory polygraph testing of certain sexual offenders', 2006, accessed January 2007, http://66.102.9.104/search?q=cache:yaX1mUmiqOQJ:www.homeoffice. gov.uk/documents/ria-manage-offenders-bill-060105/ria-offender-polygraphy-060105%3Fview%3Dbinary+Home+Office+polygraph+ testing+of+sex+offenders&hl=en&ct=clnk&cd=1&gl=uk

Home Office, National Offender Management Service website, 2007, accessed July 2007, http://noms.homeoffice.gov.uk/protecting-the-public/ risk-assessment/

Home Office, *Review of the Protection From Sex Offenders*, June 2007, London: HMSO

Home Office Task Force on Child Protection on the Internet, 'Good practice models and guidance for the internet industry on: Chat services; instant messages; web based services', accessed 10 November 2007, http://police.homeoffice.gov.uk/news-and-publications/publication/ operational-policing/ho_model.pdf?view=Binary

Home Secretary's (John Reid) Annual Speech to the Parole Board, May 2006, http://press.homeoffice.gov.uk/Speeches/sp-annual-parole-board-05-06

House of Lords, *Management of Offenders and Sentencing Bill (HL): Explanatory Notes*, 2005, accessed November 2006, www.publications. parliament.uk/pa/ld200405/ldbills/016/en/05016x--.htm

Institute of Mental Health Law Bulletin, 'Summary of reviews, inquiries and news', 2004, accessed November 2006, http://216.239.59.104/ search?q=cache:X6mu1H1UZKwJ:www.zitotrust.co.uk/IMHLSept2004. doc+%E2%80%9CI+accept+that+this+is+not+without+controversy,% E2%80%9D+the+home+secretary+writes.+%E2%80%9CGiven+the+ controversial+nature+of+these+proposals,+I+am+consulting+Peter+ Goldsmith.%E2%80%9D&hl=en&ct=clnk&cd=1&gl=uk&client= firefox-a

Johnson, B and Connolly, K, 'Britons under investigation in global internet paedophile ring', *Guardian*, 8 February 2007

Krone, T, 'A typology of online child pornography offending', *Trends and Issues in Crime and Criminal Justice*, 279 (2004), Canberra: Australian Institute of Criminology

Lameyre, X, '*La Criminalite Sexualle*', 2000, Paris: Flamarion

Laurenson, J, 'France tests "chemical castration"', 8 January 2005, Deutsche Welle, accessed February 2007, www.dw-world.de/dw/article/0,1564,145 1581,00.html

Mair, G, 'Research on community penalties', in King, R and Wincup, E (eds), *Doing Research on Crime and Justice*, 2000, Oxford: Oxford University Press

Marshall, W L, Laws, D R and Barbaree, H E, *Handbook of Sexual Assault: Issues, Theories, and Treatment of the Offender*, 1990, New York: Garland

Marshall, W L, Serran, G A, Fernandez, Y M, Mulloy, R, Mann, R E and Thornton, D, 'Therapist characteristics in the treatment of sex offenders: Tentative data on their relationship with indices of behaviour change', *Journal of Sexual Agression*, 9 (2003), p 1

National Probation Service, 'Launch of new internet sex offender treatment programme', Probation Circular, 92, 2005

Northern Ireland Office, 'Reforming the law on sexual offences in Northern Ireland: A consultation document', 2, July 2006, NI Sex Crime Unit

NSPCC 'Polygraph testing: Polygraph testing of sex offenders', 2007, accessed July 2007, http://216.239.59.104/search?q=cache:zGm34H51Lv wJ:www.nspcc.org.uk/Inform/PolicyAndPublicAffairs/Consultations/ 2006/child_sex_offender_review_gf41673.pdf+Polygraph+testing+Don+ Grubin&hl=en&ct=clnk&cd=20&gl=uk&client=firefox-a

O'Brien, M D and Webster, S D, 'The construction and preliminary validation of the internet behaviours and attitudes questionnaire', unpublished paper 2006, *Offending Behaviour Programmes Unit*, HM Prison Service

O'Connell, R, *A Typology of Child Cybersexploitation and Online Grooming Practice*, 2003, accessed October 2006, www.once.uclan.ac.uk/print/deception_print.htm

Parliamentary Research Paper, 'The Sexual Offences Act 2003', 2005, accessed December 2006, www.parliament.uk/commons/lib/research/rp200505-019.pdf

Proctor, E and Flaxington, F, 'Community based interventions with sex offenders organised by the Probation Service', 1996, Association of Chief Officers of Probation, Unpublished paper

Quakers in Britain, accessed May 2007, www.quaker.org.uk/Templates/Internal.asp?NodeID=92382

Quayle, E and Taylor, M, 'Paedophiles, pornography and the internet: Assessment issues', *British Journal of Social Work*, 32 (2002), pp 863–75

Quayle, E and Taylor, M, 'Model of problematic internet use in people with a sexual interest in children', *Cyberpsychology and Behaviour*, 6(1) (2003), pp 93–106

Risk Management Authority, 'Risk assessment tools evaluation directory', 2006, www.rmascotland.gov.uk/rmapublications.aspx

Salter, A, *Treating Child Sex Offenders and Victims: A Practical Guide*, 1988, California: Sage

Sentencing Advisory Panel, 'Sexual Offences Act 2003: The panel's advice to the Sentencing Guidelines Council', 2004, accessed February 2007, www.sentencingguidelines.gov.uk/docs/advice-sexual-offences.pdf

Seto, M C and Eke, A W, 'The criminal histories and later offending of child pornography offenders', *Sexual Abuse: A Journal of Research and Treatment*, 17(2) (2005a), pp 201–10

Seto, M C and Eke, A W, 'Extending the follow up of child pornography offenders', 2005b, unpublished paper

Strano, M, 'A neural network applied to criminal psychological profiling: An Italian initiative', *International Journal of Offender Therapy and Comparative Criminology*, 48 (2004), pp 495–503

Thornton, D, Mann, R, Webster, S, Blud, L, Travers, R and Friendship, C, 'Distinguishing and combining risks for sexual and violent recidivism', *Annals of the New York Academy of Sciences*, 989 (2003), pp 225–35

United States Bill of Rights, accessed December 2006, www.archives.gov/national-archives-experience/charters/bill_of_rights_transcript.html

Ward, T and Siegert, R J, 'Toward a comprehensive theory of child sexual abuse: A theory knitting perspective', *Crime and Law*, 8 (2002), pp 319–51

Weiss, P, 'Assessment and treatment of sex offenders in the Czech Republic and in Eastern Europe', *Journal of Interpersonal Violence*, 14(4) (1999), pp 411–21

Wright, G, 'True or false?', *Guardian*, 28 May 2004

Conclusion

Images and definitions of childhood: children as victims and yobs

Definitions and images of child sexual abuse remain problematic where there is confusion regarding the age at which childhood commences and how children and young people are to be viewed. The age of consent to sexual relations is 16 in the UK, while the age of criminal responsibility is set at ten in England and Wales and eight in Scotland. However, under certain circumstances young people are viewed as vulnerable children until the age of 18; note for example the raising of the age of consent to under 18 where the perpetrator occupies a position of trust (Sexual Offences (Amendment) Act 2003). This definition is in keeping with the EU Convention on the Rights of the Child. The age of consent varies between 14 and 16 in Europe.

There are clearly contradictions built in to legal and social definitions of childhood. Social policy becomes punitive where children are viewed as perpetrators; the media image is then of young adults who lack parental discipline, a group of unruly youth who constitute a threat to the social order. However, the welfare apparatus that has developed around the protection of young people and child victims suggests a different, more paternal response to a vulnerable group seen to be in need of state protection and care. Media commentary and imagery makes a marked distinction between the two groups: hooded, violent yobs versus defenceless victims. However, the group of young people identified as perpetrators and made to take responsibility for their offending behaviour are also the most socially deprived and vulnerable children, and probably the most likely to be victimised and to have suffered abuse.

There is also a certain hypocrisy associated with a society that condones the sexualisation of children appearing in fashion magazines and on the television, but condemns the sexual abuse of children and young people. In a recent paper Emma Rush and LaNauze (2006) from the Australian Institute suggest that companies which use sexualised images of children to advertise goods are guilty of 'corporate paedophilia' – Rush further claims that such images encourage sex offenders to view children as sexual objects. An inquiry has recently been launched by the British Fashion Council (March 2007) to explore health concerns regarding models in the fashion industry; an ex-model (Clarke, 2007) commenting in the *Daily Mail* newspaper has claimed that the review, chaired by Baroness Kingsmill, will do little to change entrenched, damaging industry practices and the use of young models. Clarke comments that the industry's obsession with very thin, childlike models, sometimes as young as 12, who are posed in sexualised images, does little to discourage the sexual abuse of young people and serves as an active endorsement of such abuse.

The Sexual Offences Act 2003 (England and Wales) appears to make a stand against the abuse of children, while successive Children Acts (1998, 2004) have built upon the EU Convention in emphasising the rights of the child. There are no simple solutions, but criminal justice policy must adopt a more consistent and rounded perspective on childhood. It is clear from victim's accounts that the experience of childhood abuse is frequently damaging and long term; research in victimology increasingly bears testament to this. It is also clear that official estimates of the extent of child sexual abuse conceal the extent of the problem, as do criminal statistics regarding the sentencing of perpetrators. Victim studies probably provide a more accurate picture, but are reliant upon victim's willingness to disclose abuse. It seems clear that 'sexual offending against children is a serious and widespread problem . . . the majority of which goes unreported' (Morrison et al., 1994, p 1) and therefore undetected. The recognition of the significance and scale of the problem is a progressive step, but it is equally important to acknowledge that children and young people who perpetrate crimes are often themselves vulnerable and are deserving of understanding and support, rather than condemnation. Society should realise that many young perpetrators may also be victims.

Child abuse inquiries, media response and government policy: failures in child protection

Successive child abuse inquiries, structured around key cases, have contributed to changes in government policy and child protection practice. However, few reported cases involving the sexual abuse of children result in a criminal conviction. Children have reported that the experience of being 'protected' by services was at times more traumatic than the alleged abuse (Jensen et al., 2005; Mudaly and Goddard, 2006). It is necessary for children to be briefed about professionals' actions in order to understand the process. This may reflect not only on the investigative process per se, but also on the number of different practitioners involved, the length of time taken for proceedings and the understanding of steps in the process. It would seem that many children and young people have been consistently 'let down' by social care agencies charged with their welfare, and that when young victims find the courage to report abuse the chances of that allegation being prosecuted and resulting in a criminal conviction are small.

One key factor emerging from research is a lack of effective inter-agency communication: there seems to be little point in encouraging children to voice an opinion, or to report abuse, if the agencies concerned with their social welfare, protection and access to justice are unable to communicate on basic issues, a point made by Laming (2005) and Victoria Climbie's father (2005). Eileen Munro (2004) suggests that there are significant failures in communication among child protection agencies that are attributable to shortcomings in professional's training, skill levels and resourcing, and that these issues will not be addressed through the creation of the child database. Munro further claims that the introduction of the database will have a detrimental effect, being expensive to implement and maintain; possibly inaccurate given the amount of detailed information to be stored; and combining information about vulnerable children with children not considered to be at risk. It may also impact negatively upon relationships between agencies and parents when the extent to which privacy is invaded is realised, and may conceal real concerns and lead to further agency inaction. Research conducted by the author with child protection police officers supports this contention, and suggests further that staff retention and decreased resourcing over successive years are having a demoralising effect on staff (Davidson et al., 2007). While there is agreement that inter-agency communication must improve, it seems that the national database proposal may lead to agencies drowning in information, which may be inaccurate and will not address under-lying fundamental issues around the training and retention of staff and the resourcing of child protection social care and criminal justice agencies.

Images and perceptions of abusers: key cases and social policy

In the aftermath of heightened media coverage of isolated cases involving the abduction and murder of children, government meas-ures to control and manage this group of offenders, all of whom are now inextricably linked with Roy Whiting and Ian Huntley in the public imagination, have become ever more desperate and legislation has become increasingly punitive. Research suggests that low self-esteem, relationship problems and social isolation are enduring features in the lives of these (predominantly male) offenders, often exacerbated by their conviction and labelling as 'child molesters'. Given public and media concern over this issue, it is in reality increasingly difficult for these offenders to ever conduct an ordinary daily existence in society. The tension here is between the importance of providing a safe environment for children and protecting the civil liberties of this group, many of whom, unlike any other groups of offenders, will be tracked and publicly identified long after they have completed their custodial or community sentence (and in some cases for the rest of their lives). This is not to deny the impact of such offending upon victims, but it must be recognised that the vast majority of sex offenders subject to the restrictions of the sex offender register are categorised as low risk. There are no simple solutions to this problem.

Sentencing policy and practice

The Labour Government's response to the wave of media criticism regarding the sentencing and management of sex offenders has been to introduce increasingly punitive legislation that seeks to punish and control these offenders, both in custody and in the community, while at the same time attempting to provide public reassurance regarding 'risk' of re-offending. Some have argued that such moves have done little to reintegrate such offenders into society following release from prison, and have served to limit employment opportunities (Brown et al., 2007).

Legislation in both the UK and Australia allows sentencers to pass 'indeterminate' sentences where risk of re-offending is considered high. Attempts to place growing restrictions on sex offenders are not restricted to the UK. Lieb (2000) suggests that the US Government, and increasingly EU Governments, are focusing upon methods outside of criminal law to control sex offender populations. In the United States many sex offenders, who have completed their prison sentences, remain incarcerated in psychiatric institutions due to 'indefinite civil commitment' rulings. This enables sentencers to imprison sex offenders indefinitely where some evidence of mental disorder that indicates ongoing risk is produced. The psychiatric profession have questioned the wisdom of incarcerating large numbers of sex offenders in mental health institutions and the definition of mental health problems that form the basis of their further detention. Nineteen states have adopted the controversial legislation, and detention facilities are expanding. States are being actively financially encouraged by the US Government to detain sex offenders beyond custodial sentence.

Following the US example recent legislation in the UK has sought to establish a long-term register of offenders and to endow the police with the power to track and monitor those known, or believed, to have committed sexual offences against children. Considerable media and public pressure to make information from the sex offender register available to parents has been placed upon the government following the abduction and murder of 8-year-old Sarah Payne. Sex offenders are the only group of offenders in British legal history to have designated acts and civil orders. The move to simultaneously punish and control this offender group has developed, alongside an effort on the part of criminal justice agencies such as the Prison Service and the Probation Service, to provide effective treatment programmes. Rehabilitation should be a primary aim of criminal justice policy with this offender group, however, while the worth of treatment is recognised, the paradigm of sex offender social control is now firmly fixed upon the need to identify the 'dangerous' or 'potentially dangerous', assess their risk level and deal with them as effectively as possible, before they are able to perpetrate further harm and in a way that satisfies public anxiety.

Managing the risk and actuarial measures: public reassurance

The responsibility of 'protecting the public from serious harm' posed by child sexual abusers in the real world and in cyberspace is a difficult one: such offences are shrouded in secrecy; offenders often effectively conceal abuse; victims are often reluctant to report abuse and consequently offences are under-reported. Attempts to control, manage, treat and predict re-offending are fraught with difficulties, and any mistakes involving the commission of further sexual offences against children will be played out in the full glare of the media spotlight. Practitioners working with such difficult offenders are charged with the responsibility of accurately predicting the risk they pose and with their rehabilitation. This work occurs in the context of MAPPA arrangements and measures, such as polygraph testing and satellite tracking, introduced by the Home Office to place restrictions upon sex offender's behaviour in the community.

A lot of good developmental work has been undertaken by practitioners working with child abusers, but the risk such offenders pose is not diminished by the existence of risk assessment structures and processes, and can risk assessment tools really indicate likely re-offending among a group whose behaviour is erratic and unpredictable? At least if re-offending occurs the responsible criminal justice agency can claim that risk assessment and management protocol was followed; the re-offending then becomes 'accidental' and not a consequence of agency incompetence or ineptitude. This view is supported by Ward and Siegert (2002) who have argued that criminal justice decision-making is becoming increasingly 'risk' based. It is suggested that the Probation Service, driven by the Home Office, has placed a great deal of energy and funding into the development of processes for managing risk and continues to search for increasingly accurate risk measurement tools, as if in some way the ability to quantify risk validates decisions made by practitioners regarding offenders. Ward and Siegert (op. cit.) argue that the Probation Service would do better to open a dialogue with the community about offender re-integration and risk, exploring levels of community tolerance to risk and re-offending. It is suggested that the government and criminal justice agencies should recognise that risk cannot always be accurately predicted. This is a good suggestion, but it seems that the Probation Service and other criminal justice agencies charged with the management of serious offenders should, as Ward suggests, open a more honest dialogue with communities in recognising that a minority of serious offenders are highly likely to re-offend and in reality, although systems are in place, it is very difficult to risk assess, monitor and control this group in the community.

It could be argued that a paradigm shift is occurring within criminal justice, and that a systems analysis approach to danger management of offenders has come to characterise policy and practice (Feeley and Simon, 1992, 1994). In this 'new penology' the focus is actuarial and concern is not with punishment or rehabilitation, but with the classification of offenders by seriousness of offence and risk posed.

This model applies particularly to attempts to manage sex offenders both in the United States, UK and other EU countries where the emphasis is upon ways to maximise the control of offenders, and as Garland suggests '(sex) offenders are viewed as *risks who must be managed*. Instead of emphasizing rehabilitative methods that meet the offender's needs, the system emphasises effective controls that minimize costs and maximize security' (Garland, 2001, p 175). Actuarial risk assessment tools play a significant part in this process, allowing criminal justice practitioners to calculate the risk posed and determine both sentence and treatment on this basis. In the United States such tools also serve to justify the long-term incarceration of sex offenders subject to indefinite civil commitment orders.

Concluding comments

This book has explored the definition, policy and social context of child sexual abuse, considering both the position of child victims and approaches to offender punishment and control. Child abuse is a newsworthy subject; it has been suggested that media representation of key child abuse cases and inquiries such as Cleveland, Waterhouse, Climbie and Bichard has been instrumental in shaping negative public perceptions of agencies involved in child protection and of perpetrators. Legislative measures have often been introduced swiftly in response to media coverage and perceived public concern. Measures such as the child database, designed to improve inter-agency communication in the aftermath of the Climbie Inquiry, and the proposed disclosure of sex offender details to selected members of the public, will in reality do little to address the underlying causes of and incidence of abuse, most of which is perpetrated by individuals known to children, often within families.

In the relentless drive to name and shame, risk assess, manage, categorise, chemically castrate and demonise abusers, it is possible to forget that child sexual abuse is a serious social problem that damages children. This drive is conducted in the name of child protection, but it is too easy to lose sight of the victim in this process: when children and young people do find the courage to report abuse and recount their experiences, the difficulties inherent in an adult adversarial system that is predicated upon the production of consistent and systematic evidence, results in investigative practice that is not designed to elicit the best from children and consequently many withdraw.

Despite the efforts of many dedicated child protection practitioners, training budgets remain small, inter-agency collaboration problematic, staff turnover high and morale low. Police officers have suggested that despite the recent dearth of government measures addressing sex offender control, in reality child protection remains a low priority and that budgets in this area have been cut consistently year after year.[1] It is right to develop measured, evidenced and humane approaches to sex offender treatment and management, but focus and resourcing must also be levelled firmly at the victim in the investigative process, in exploring why it is that so many child sexual abuse cases are never prosecuted.

References

Brown, K, Spencer, J and Deakin, J, 'The reintegration of sex offenders: barriers and opportunities for employment', *Howard Journal of Criminal Justice*, 46(1) (2007), pp 32–42

Clarke, G, 'They measured my fingers to see if I was fat', *Daily Mail*, 29 May 2007

Climbie, J, 'Key Climbie recommendations still not implemented', *Daily Mail*, 22 May 2006, accessed October 2006, www.dailymail.co.uk/pages/live/articles/news/news.html?in_article_id=387182&in_page_id=1770

Davidson, J, Bifulco, A, Thomas, G and Ramsey, M, 'Placing the child at the centre of police practice and procedure: First stage final report to the Metropolitan Police Child Abuse Investigation Command', 2007, University of Westminster; Royal Holloway, University of London, London

---

1   See Davidson, Bifulco, Thomas and Ramsey (2007).

Feeley, M and Simon, J, 'The new penology: Notes on the emerging strategy of corrections and its implications', *Criminology*, 30 (1992), pp 449–74

Feeley, M and Simon, J, 'Actuarial justice: The emerging new criminal law', in Nelken, D (ed), *The Futures of Criminology*, 1994, London: Sage

Garland, D, *The Culture of Control: Crime and Social Order in Contemporary Society*, 2001, Oxford: Oxford University Press

Jensen, T K, Gulbrandson, W, Mossige, S, Reichelt, S and Tjersland, O A, 'Reporting possible sexual abuse: A qualitative study on children's perspectives and the context for disclosure', *Child Abuse and Neglect*, 29 (2005), pp 1395–413

Kingsmill, Baroness, 'British Fashion Council establishes model health inquiry, chaired by Baroness Kingsmill', Press Release, 23 March 2007, accessed July 2007, www.modelhealthinquiry.com/docs/BFC%20model%20Health%20Inquiry.pdf

Laming, Lord, opening address at the Every Child Matters Conference, 3 March 2005

Lieb, R, 'Social policy and sexual offenders: Contrasting United States and European policies', *European Journal on Criminal Policy and Research*, 8(4) (2000), pp 423–40

Morrison, T, Erooga, M and Beckett, R, *Sexual Offending Against Children*, 1994, London: Routledge

Mudaly, N and Goddard, C, *The Truth is Longer than a Lie: Children's Experiences of Abuse and Professional Interventions*, 2006, Jessica Kingsley: London

Munro, E, 'Memorandum Submitted to United Kingdom Parliament Select Committee on Education and Skills', Minutes of Evidence, 2004, pp 1–3

Rush, E and La Nauze, A, *Corporate Paedophilia: Sexualisation of Children in Australia*, 2006, Canberra: Australia Institute

The Victoria Climbie Inquiry, Report of an Inquiry by Lord Laming, 2003, accessed November 2006, www.victoria-climbie-inquiry.org.uk/finreport/finreport.htm

Ward, T and Siegert, R J, 'Toward a comprehensive theory of child sexual abuse: A theory knitting perspective', *Crime and Law*, 8 (2002), pp 319–51

Index